Reaching Out

Reaching Out

Rainette Bannister Holimon

Writer's Showcase
San Jose New York Lincoln Shanghai

Reaching Out

Writer's Showcase
an imprint of iUniverse.com, Inc.

For information address:
iUniverse.com, Inc.
5220 S 16th, Ste. 200
Lincoln, NE 68512
www.iuniverse.com

ISBN: 0-595-16805-1

Printed in the United States of America

FOR   *MAMA*
                                   TED
                                   MARLENE
                                   MILDRED

Preface

I suppose I first started thinking about Africa after a brief discussion with my mother. During the course of a general conversation, Mama said to me, "Papa's people came from Malagasy, having been victims of the slave trade". (This country is now called Madagascar. Papa's people would be my great-grandfather's descendants. I was surprised, but really took no further follow-through on this remark. This was before the surging interest in Africa, before the violent 60s, before the wide display of African fabrics and various other items that one sees today. Nevertheless, this African revelation settled within me, almost unknowingly, almost as if I had stored it away in a memory bank to be opened later.

In 1973, I took a brief vacation to Nairobi, Kenya, East Africa. When I arrived, I was not only overwhelmed by the mass of Black people, but also devastated by the signs of abject poverty.

Upon my return from vacation, and after many weeks of meditation, I began thinking about the U.S. Peace Corps. I had been working for AT&T Bell Laboratories since 1964. Prior to that I had worked for twenty years with the Federal government. Why give up this and go in the Peace Corps? Most of all, I was fed up with the corporate world, the "dog-eat-dog" system, the values that everyone seemed to place on their lifestyles, the materialistic concepts, the greed. I felt as if I could be reaching out and serving a much better purpose in life by helping other people in the less developed countries. I was truly appalled at the conditions that I had seen in Africa. I had no idea that "freedom" had just brought the people that, "freedom" only, without ways and means and wherewithal to survive. I had already, over the past twenty years, expended much of my energy in the United States helping the young and the old through teaching, counseling, and care-giving. It was time for a change, not a permanent one, but a chance to serve in a broader and more rewarding sense; a chance to reach out and make a difference.

I requested, and eventually received, an Educational Leave of Absence from Bell Laboratories in order to join the Peace Corps. I was accepted and, to my surprise and delight, was given an assignment in Nairobi, Kenya! Was it coincidental or had fate just destined me back to this country? Kenya was my first international venture. Later, I was to spend an exciting but fearful period in Tehran, Iran with a corporate company, and another eventful and turbulent period as a Peace Corps volunteer again, in Sierra Leone, West Africa.

I believe that reaching out to people in other lands has enabled me to truly gain complete fulfillment in life. My journeys in Africa, especially, were of such tremendous significance to me, so much so that I consider Africa my second "home". I can honestly say that I cherish these African ventures as the best years of my life.

Acknowledgments

There are many people whom I would like to thank for helping me put this book together, including a few who have passed on, but who will never be forgotten.

Firstly, heartfelt thanks to Mary Jane Otto, former Peace Corps volunteer and English teacher. My "right hand" when we served together at the National Youth Service Secretarial School in Kenya, East Africa. Without her support and teachings, our Peace Corps venture would not have been such a success.

Special thanks and blessings to Simon Peter Mburu, my Kenyan counterpart, for his perseverance and everlasting friendship.

Of course, I can never express more profoundly my deep appreciation to the late Mildred Boyd, my former supervisor, for her concerted efforts and success with the donation of electric typewriters for our school; and in this connection, the support of AT&T Bell Laboratories which made Mildred's efforts possible.

Many thanks to a dear friend, the late Jules Godsey, graphics designer. I will always remember the posters that Jules prepared and sent to me when we first set up the school classrooms.

Gratefulness to Ambassador Cynthia S. Perry, and Dr. James O. Perry, my friends whose home I made my "home away from home" while in Kenya. Without their warmth and kindness during my time in Africa, I am sure I would not have overcome the many obstacles that I encountered.

Special thanks to those who actually visited me in Kenya, Carol and Tony Rustako, Sheila and Marvin Wiggins, David and Marilyn Carson, my everlasting friend, Marshall Schachtman, and, of course, my late husband, Theodore Holimon.

Acknowledgments and remembrances are endless to those many friends and relatives who supported me throughout my ventures. I am forever grateful for their letters and care packages. Namely, Edward (Ebbie) Thomas, Virginia Dickerson, Dorothy Taylor and the late Robert Taylor, Christine and Mack Owens and Nana, Bertha (Bootsie) Mills, the late Otis (Sacks) Simms, and my late sister and brother-in-law, Betty and Johnny Dickerson.

Many thanks to the late Roland Webb and the late Lenora Walker McKay, both who wrote and published their own books. Their advice was most helpful when I contemplated writing this book. Thanks to Lionel Wilson for his interest and suggestions. Special thanks to Carole Dortch-Wright for helping me with the title and offering her professional critique.

Kudos to my friend George Watson, one of the original Tuskegee Airmen. Having written a book himself, George was able to offer countless suggestions and steered me in the right direction.

Blessings forever to Drs. Kenneth Nahum, James W. Knecht, and Mark Ornstein. Also for the tender loving care received from nurses Kathy, Deborah, and the late Delores Mohammed, all whom I consider my medical angels when I survived a serious illness upon my return from Sierra Leone.

Accolades to my grand-niece, Kim Robinson, for her endless typing and retyping of my original manuscript, plus her patience in trying to teach me how to master the "Apple". Thanks, also, to my niece, Liz Goldsmith for proofreading the final manuscript and making positive suggestions.

Special accolades to my computer consultants, Roberto Royale, Winifred Johnson, and My grandnephew, Richard "Flip" Suit, for their patience, fortitude, and expertise when assisting me with the final stages of my manuscript.

Again, thanks to any and all friends who, although not mentioned here, I am sure you were "with me" throughout my many trials and tribulations.

Contents

List of Illustrations

PART ONE
Kenya

First Peace Corps Venture

1

My first international work experience began in Nairobi, Kenya, East Africa, in August, 1974. When I applied for Peace Corps service, I specifically requested that I be assigned to an African country. After many weeks of correspondence, loads of forms and paperwork, numerous telephone calls, a complete physical, and basic planning, I was accepted by the United States Peace Corps.

In late August 1974, I reported to Washington, DC for three days of orientation and processing. It was understood that after these three days, I would continue on to East Africa with no return home until after my two years of service with Peace Corps were completed.

The orientation in Washington consisted basically of audio and visual aids to give the volunteers a feel for the kind of lifestyle we would be subjected to in a Third World country. The orientation group which I participated in consisted of myself, one white male and three white females. The male volunteer was designated for an Up-Country (Bush) area outside of Nairobi. The rest of us were assigned to a small town named Ruaraka, located approximately seven miles outside the capital, Nairobi. In Ruaraka we were to be joined by another volunteer (white female) who was already there on assignment.

While in Washington, the Peace Corps informed me that my role as volunteer would be that of principal of a secretarial school that was just starting in Ruaraka. The other four volunteers would serve as teachers of English, commerce, shorthand, and typewriting. I would also teach an office practice course in addition to my duties as principal.

After completion of our orientation, we departed for Kenya. The flight to Kenya was on the ole Pan-Am "Red-Eye"—approximately 23 hours flying time with seven stops! Needless to say, the flight was long and strenuous. At one point, we encountered a terrific storm, and the pilot had to climb way above the clouds to escape some of the heavy turbulence. As I peered below, in the darkness, I could see sharp lightning so bright and widespread that it looked like a battlefield!

The approach to Kenya was breathtaking! As the plane descended, I could see the beautiful Kenya sunrise, and I was fortunate enough to capture this on film (see Cover). And then we finally landed! The hustle and bustle at the airport was exciting. I was amazed to see so many people throughout the airport, loading and unloading baggage, some speaking English, some speaking Swahili, and many speaking other languages. But what struck me most was that all of these people were black! At last, I thought, I am finally in a majority population with my people!

After endless hours of waiting for our luggage, we emerged from the baggage area and were met by members of the Peace Corps staff who were already stationed in Kenya. From the airport we went to the home of one of the Peace Corps staff members, Dennis Danchik.

Here we were treated to a delicious meal of fresh fruits, chicken and beef, a Kikuyu dish called irio (consisting of beans and corn), ugali (cooked maize similar to hominy grits, and fresh greens (sukuma wiki). Imagine my surprise when I realized the sukuma wiki was my old home favorite, collard greens. Sukuma wiki is a Swahili word meaning, "push the week." The Kenyan family often survived on sukuma wiki alone, literally, "pushing the week" with these greens when there was no other food available. During my entire stay in Kenya, I learned to like the irio and ugali, and of course, always relied on my favorite sukuma wiki.

Here I would like to give a bit of background about the organization which I had been assigned to by Peace Corps. This organization was called the National Youth Service. The creation of the National Youth Service, a paramilitary organization, was among the very first acts of independent Kenya, the decision stemming from late 1965, when Kenya achieved full independence. At that time, women's vocational programs were limited to agriculture, dressmaking, driver training, and various types of construction.

The purpose of the National Youth Service was to train young citizens to serve the nation and to provide its members with vocational skills. In stressing this purpose, His Excellency, Jomo Kenyatta, the President of Kenya, wanted the young people who enlisted in the National Youth Service to dedicate two years of their lives to their country. This dedication was to be given without thoughts of personal reward other than the knowledge that the work they accomplished would be a positive and tangible contribution to the rapid, economic, political, and social advancement of Kenya.

Various training institutions were set up throughout Kenya, and the National Youth Service Secretarial School was one of these institutions. The secretarial school was to be the largest training program for the female members of the National Youth Service. These women had volunteered to serve their country for a minimum of two years. They came from all parts of Kenya, and ranged in age from sixteen to twenty-three years.

Prior to taking on our official assignment at the secretarial school, the five of us, along with other volunteers, were given six weeks of Swahili language training. Although English is spoken throughout Kenya and used in the school, Swahili is the lingua franca. We were sent to Mombasa for our language classes. Mombasa is a beautiful coastal city in Kenya. The climate there was very hot and humid, compared to Nairobi, which has a more temperate climate, even to the point of sometimes being actually very cool. The town is much smaller than Nairobi. The Muslim influence is evidenced by the many mosques throughout the city and the sound of the daily religious call to prayer. In spite of the heat, the coastal beauty is so breathtaking, and the view of the sun coming up early in the morning overshadows any discomfort one might have.

Our Swahili classes lasted four to five hours a day. The instructors were Kenyans, all very skillful in their mastery of the Swahili language. The language was difficult for me, and I regret to say that I never did master it to fluency. The fact that we were allowed to speak

English probably hampered my learning to some extent. Also, even though the classes were conducted in Swahili, once classes were over we quickly reverted back to English. And, of course, our classes at the secretarial school were conducted solely in English with no Swahili permitted at all. Upon completion of our language training in Mombasa, we returned to Nairboi and were housed at a local hotel in the city. We were then given the arduous task of trying to find individual housing accommodations.

Prior to finding housing accommodations, however, and as part of our training, each one of us was housed with a Kenyan family. The main purpose of this was to give the volunteer some feeling about the poverty in the country, and to experience living under hard, strenuous conditions. Some of the volunteers did undergo difficult situations during this period. I, however, was housed with a moderate income family and underwent no sacrifices whatsoever. I was extremely disappointed with this, since I really wanted to experience "Bush" living, but I had no choice in Peace Corps' decision.

My family consisted of Mr. and Mrs. Kombo and their two children, ages 6 and 8. The home was newly constructed and contained all the modern conveniences one would expect to see in the States. The Kombos were both college graduates and had spent considerable time living in the United States.

While I lived with the Kombos, the other three volunteers were housed in more rural homes. I could sense that they resented the fact that I had more convenient accommodations.

When I was given this assignment in Kenya, I had no previous knowledge of the other volunteers' qualifications or backgrounds. Little did I dream that problems would arise and that the "ole devil, racism" would erupt so quickly upon my arrival in East Africa.

I lived with the Kenya family for a period of one week, then returned to the local hotel until I found suitable housing. Although Peace Corps would pay for our housing, we had the physical task of finding our own accommodations. In doing so, however, we had to stay within a certain cost limit. Nairobi is a relatively modern city with numerous homes and apartment buildings for rent. There were no housing facilities near the school in Ruaraka, thus Nairobi was our only choice. There were many homes available in the surrounding suburbs of Nairobi, however, these areas were quite expensive. Also, these facilities were mainly occupied by Europeans and other foreigners who were working and living in Kenya. The average Kenyan could not afford these facilities. During this period, most of the Kenyans lived on the outskirts of Nairobi in poorly constructed buildings.

After a few weeks of searching, I was able to find a small cottage in an area called Westlands. This cottage had once been used as a guest house. The large front house was owned and occupied by a European business-man and his family. He had converted the guest house into a cottage for rent. The cottage was small and unpretentious. It had a tiny kitchen area, a small sitting room, and a small bedroom in the basement area. It was suitable for my needs, and, in fact, could be considered a mansion compared to the way many of the Africans lived.

There was a small shopping area which catered to the European population. Because of this, I had access to all the basic, fine butcher shops and grocery shops. The Africans who worked in the area or lived in the rural towns a few miles from Westlands, did their shopping at a small open market near the regular shopping area.

The sparseness of my home was compensated for by the beauty of the bougainvillea that surrounded my "hut." I slept in the basement area for a short period, but because of its dampness and constant invasion of large, black spiders, I eventually had my bed moved upstairs to the sitting room area. After weeks of spraying away the spiders, I finally settled down in my new home.

Living in Westlands was quite a distance from transportation facilities to the secretarial school. First, I had to walk a mile to the first bus stop. From there I took a bus to the local bus station, and from the bus station took another bus to my school site. The buses were always crowded. Sometimes there was seating, sometimes standing room only. All of the city buses usually carried at least 100 passengers—43 seated, 57 standing. This, coupled with passengers carrying bags of maize, potatoes, rice, green vegetables, and very often live chickens, made the bus rides quite tight and uncomfortable. And, of course, there was always a young "mama" with a baby on her back.

The amazing strength of the Africans, both male and female is phenomenal. Sometimes a bus would break down on the road. Then all of the passengers would alight and help the bus driver by pushing the bus until it started up again. Very often the bus was on an incline, but still the passengers would help. Then everyone would climb back on the bus. As one can imagine, I was a frequent bystander when the pushing of the bus began.

I recall once seeing four men lift a four-passenger sedan out of a ditch onto level ground. They gripped the car on all sides, gave the initial call of "harambee" ("pull together") and picked up the car with seemingly little difficulty.

And the women! Every morning, from my school window, I would see women going to the forest to chop and gather wood for their homes. They were carrying machetes, axes, water jugs and other paraphernalia. Then later, around noon, I would see them coming back, laden with this wood they had chopped, going home to make fires and cook for their families, plus nurse their children. These women were not really old, but looked aged because of the hard work and struggles they endured.

Labeling the African as lazy, which is done so often by the media in other countries, is certainly unfounded and a misnomer.

THE LONG WALK HOME

WOMEN CARRYING WOOD FROM THE FOREST

The National Youth Service Secretarial School

2

The top Kenyan officials in charge of the entire National Youth Service consisted of the director, Mr. G. W. Griffin, the deputy director, Mr. Waruhiu Itote ("General China"). the assistant director, Mr. C. Githaiga, the training director, Mr. Owitti, and Mr. Gower. A note of interest concerning deputy director Itote. If the reader is familiar with the Mau Mau struggle that took place during the bloody liberation of Kenya in the 1950s, it should bring to mind the vital role General China played in Kenya's struggle for independence. He and other experienced soldiers were instrumental in leading African warriors into the Aberdare forest where they were trained to become good soldiers. Mr. Gower was a European who worked side by side with the director in the formation of the secretarial school.

After Kenya received its independence, the National Youth Service was one of the first organizations formed for the revitalization of Kenya. General China was appointed deputy director of the National Youth Service. In this position, he played an important role in the formation of the secretarial school.

The secretarial school was designed to give a second chance to young women who had been unable to make their way up through formal education. The aim of the school was to teach these women from rural areas basic business skills, and thus enable them to obtain more meaningful and gainful employment. Many of these women were previously enrolled in one of the other National Youth Service programs, i.e., driver training, agriculture, and dressmaking. Before being accepted into the secretarial school, however, all of these women had completed a basic training program.

The women who attended the secretarial school were housed at the National Youth Service compound located just a short distance from the school. They were given board, food, uniforms, and a meager monthly allowance. From this allowance the women had to pay school fees to attend the secretarial school. This allowance also had to cover their personal needs.

The secretarial school consisted of a long, wooden building that had once been the original National Youth Service Headquarters. It had been renovated and made into three classrooms, the principal's office, a reception area, and a small lounge for the teaching staff. Small toilet facilities were also available. We were equipped with electricity, running water, and a telephone that was frequently out of order. Although the school was plain and unpretentious, we, the teaching staff, were satisfied with our surroundings.

Before the secretarial school officially opened, the five of us participated in a basic training program for a period of two weeks at the school. The training and orientation consisted mainly of cultural orientation sessions conducted by Kenyans under the jurisdiction of the Peace Corps. We were fortunate to have an American consultant, Dr. Cynthia S. Perry, a professional, who was proficient in international development and foreign affairs. (Dr. Perry was later to become an Ambassador to Sierra Leone, West Africa, followed by another appointment as Ambassador to Burundi, East Central Africa).

Another consultant for Peace Corps was Mr. Joseph Kuria, a Kenyan. His main position was that of Associate Director for Peace Corps volunteers assigned to various up-country areas in Kenya. In addition, he served as a consultant for incoming volunteers new to the country of Kenya. During my entire stay in Kenya, Mr. Kuria played an important part in assisting and guiding me throughout my assignment.

As consultant for Peace Corps, Mr. Kuria introduced us to some of the customs and mores found in many African countries. Here are just a few:

1) Africans always use their right hand when greeting people, when eating, and when receiving articles from others. This custom stems from the belief that the left hand was dirty. Due to lack of modern, everyday toilet facilities that we are accustomed to in our culture, the African often had to use his left hand for wiping and cleaning purposes, particularly when attending to toilet needs. Thus a stigma was always attached to the left hand. In conjunction with this, Africans also generally eat with their hands (right hand, of course). As the African became more educated and came in contact with the business and social world, these eating customs changed to our universal way of eating, that is, with utensils. However, in most cases, when the African returns to his village or even the privacy of his own home, wherever it may be, he often reverts back to the custom of eating with his hands.

2) Toilet facilities in Kenya (and in many other countries) are quite different from those found in the western world. In the average home or hut, the toilet is located outside. The toilet is actually a large hole dug very, very deep in the ground. One has to stand or squat to use this type of toilet. Usually this hole is enclosed within a wooden frame, but sometimes it is completely open. Sometimes there is no toilet paper. After using the facility, a cup

or bucket of water nearby is used for washing one's hands and other parts of the body.

3) Lack of eye contact was another factor in African culture, particularly if the African felt that he or she was confronting a person who was in some official capacity, such as a supervisor or other authoritative figure. This was strongly evidenced with our students. In the beginning, they made no eye contact with the teachers, always lowering their heads or looking to the side. However, as we progressed in our teaching and became more acquainted with the students, this behavior changed. The students became more relaxed, but in no way did they ever become too familiar or disrespectful.

4) Another factor noticeable in the African culture was body odor. One must take into consideration that body deodorants are a luxury to the African. When it comes to the decision of whether to feed himself and his family or buy deodorants, food comes first. Besides, deodorants are extremely expensive in Africa. During the development of our teachings, we introduced personal hygiene as one of the extra subjects. As a result, when they received their monthly allowance, they began to set aside moneys for their personal needs.

Dr. Perry, our consultant, concentrated on explaining to us, as volunteers, what to expect from the students, their inhibitions, and shortcomings. She stressed the importance of not only educating the student, but also communicating with them in a favorable and positive way. We were never to assume that the students were ignorant. In many cases the students were naturally shy and inhibited, not having been exposed to Americans or to our cultural differences. Dr. Perry's expertise was overwhelming. She had traveled extensively throughout Africa and was able to express her views in a way that made our task as teachers more positive and enlightening.

Mr. Kuria also included in his cultural lectures a short synopsis about the Maasai people of Kenya. The Maasai have strived to perpetuate their original culture. They are tall, statuesque, elegant, black and beautiful. They seldom come into the cities, but when they do, they still attract the attention of not only the tourists, but also the other Kenyan cultures as well.

The staff at the secretarial school, as previously mentioned, consisted of myself , the principal, and four other female teachers. These other teachers were white Americans. At the very beginning of our training sessions, I sensed a feeling of resentment towards me by three of the members of the teaching staff (the typing, commerce, and shorthand teachers). I tried to ignore this at first, but as time passed, I realized that this resentment was due to my being a black American who had the distinction of being principal of the school. I had been exposed to this kind of resentment and racism most of my life, beginning with high school and on into my employment with the federal government and the corporate world. I knew this was not an imaginary thing. When one lives with racism as long as I have, one can actually smell it! Were it not for the strong support of the English teacher, Jane Otto, I don't know how I could have managed to succeed as well as I did. Also, I received the support of Dr. Perry who acted as an intermediary to overcome some of these racial obstacles.

Let me interject something at this point. When I applied to the Peace Corps, they had stressed the importance of a college degree and teaching experience. I later learned that the typing teacher was fresh out of high school with no teaching experience, nor did the shorthand teacher have a degree or any teaching experience. I have observed during my African experiences that white America tends to put aside certain academic requirements when recruiting whites. It is as if white America is saying that any kind of education by whites is superior when it comes to teaching Africans and other minorities, simply because they, the teachers, are white. Therefore, these educational requirements that are imposed upon me and other black Americans are often lifted when the whites are being considered. Even though this was in the early 70s when many white Americans were allowed to slip through without the education and experience demanded of the black Americans, I found this practice still in existence when, in 1990, I undertook my second Peace Corps assignment in Sierra Leone, West Africa.

Upon completion of our cultural training and orientation, we took on the task of practice teaching for one month. This was an experimental process whereby we selected a number of women from the National Youth Service and proceeded to introduce them to the fundamentals of secretarial training.

When we first started our initial training at the secretarial school, I, as principal, had to interact daily with the male population of the National Youth Service. With the exception of the director, the deputy director, and assistant deputy director, I was constantly ridiculed.

The other male personnel, who also had responsible positions within the National Youth Service, would say to me: "Principal, you are wasting your time! These girls will never learn. They will only get pregnant and have to return to their village. They will never learn how to type. They will never get jobs." More than once I had to march up to the school headquarters and confront these male chauvinists, vehemently and defiantly, to argue with them about their negative remarks. Of course, they were astonished at my behavior, not being use to a woman answering back to them.

It took many, many months before these same individuals began to realize that the "girls" were learning and that our school was going to work! But it took a lot of verbal fighting on my part to convince them!

NATIONAL YOUTH SERVICE SECRETARIAL SCHOOL

MADAM RAINETTE SCHOOL PRINCIPAL

MAASAI MAIDEN

AMERICAN TOURIST WITH MAASAI FAMILY

School Opens!

3

OCTOBER 1974!—The National Youth Service Secretarial School officially opened. Our first enrollment consisted of 67 women with varied educational backgrounds. Some only had six or seven years of elementary education. Others had schooling equivalent to one or two years of secondary education. The students were trilingual, having learned their mother tongue first, Kiswahili (the national language) second, and English, third. Some of the students also spoke the languages of other tribes. English was the medium of instruction. The first 67 students had previously performed well on the basic requirements, entrance exams and personal interviews; therefore, they were the ones chosen in our final selection.

The sight of these 67 students marching smartly down the hill from the headquarters compound was something to behold! They were dressed in their usual green uniforms, but for some reason, today, the uniforms seemed to almost sparkle. These young ladies appeared to walk more erect, their heads held high and an aura of excitement and pride surrounded them. This was truly the beginning of a significant experience for all of them.

The school had been open less than one month when I was called to headquarters by Mr. Owitti, the Training Director. He asked me to be seated, then made this statement: "Madam Principal, I have some disturbing news. We have just discovered that ten women enrolled at the secretarial school are pregnant. Consequently, they have been dismissed from the National Youth Service." He then proceeded to give me the names of the women.

Naturally, I was more than disappointed at this news, since these ten women had scored rather high on their entrance exams and we had anticipated extensive potential and success with them. At the time of my meeting with Mr. Owitti, I did think it rather strange that all ten of these very good students were pregnant. However, I accepted Mr. Owitti's story.

It was a short time later that I learned from one of the servicewomen officers that Mr. Owitti had lied to me. The officer told me that these ten women had been pulled from the school and given to the Kenya Police Department to be trained as policewomen. Some of the officials had been so impressed with the results of these women's entrance exams that they decided they would be of more service to the country as policewomen. Bear in mind, these were the same officials who had scoffed at the idea of teaching these women secretarial skills.

To this day, I am unsure as to whether the Director was aware of the circumstances which pulled these women from our school. I do know that the women had no say in the matter. Although they wanted to attend the secretarial school, they were ordered to become policewomen. This was my first experience with the subterfuge that took place with some of the officials at the National Youth Service, but it was not the last.

The first six months at the school were grueling and frustrating. The task of getting acquainted with the students by trying to understand their English, and they, in turn, trying to understand our English was a major obstacle in itself. We, as Americans, tend to speak too fast, and times our diction, that is, "d" and "t" endings leave much to be desired. With the exception of the English teacher, Jane Otto, we were a bit weak along these lines. The African, when she/he masters the English language, speaks distinctly and slowly. If nothing else, during my stay in East Africa, although my goal was to teach the students secretarial skills, I also learned a lot more about the English language just by listening to the students enunciate. Unfortunately, when I completed my assignment and returned to the United States, I fell back to the sloppy style of speaking English the way it is usually spoken in America.

In addition to overcoming the task of English communication, we also had to learn to pronounce the names of the students. In most cases the students' first names had been changed to Christian names bestowed upon them by the missionaries who were highly visible before independence. Names like Purity, Charity, Faith, Hope, and others, were common. But their real names were those of their specific ethnic background, with every name having a specific meaning. To list a few:

Wairime, Mbugwa, Kalondu, Kimani, Muthoni, Nyambura, Atieno, Nekesa, Okwempa

Ithima, Wahogo, Achieng, Acheni, Githinji, Warigui, Olimba, Thuku, Naitore, Mbone, Gaceri, Kagori, Miginjo, Adhiambo, Wanjiku, Wanjiru, Apiyo, Wambui, Njeri, Kinuthia, Mwawasi, Mbuvi, Zakayo, Maina, Kimana, Gatheru, and on and on.

As our classes progressed, the students and teachers became familiar with each other. Since the English teacher was so experienced and proficient in the teaching field, I soon recommended to the Director that Madam Jane be appointed Assistant Principal. I submitted my recommendation, and in February, 1975, the appointment was made. It proved to be a wise decision, since Madam Jane became my "right hand" during our time spent together at the secretarial school.

The biggest obstacle and challenge during the first six months at the school, however, was the hostile behavior and attitude of the other three American Peace Corps volunteers. They went out of their way to be uncooperative. The typing teacher was young and totally inexperienced, and her performance showed it. Her academic skills were limited. The commerce teacher, although academically qualified, also evidenced resentment of my position. The shorthand teacher was so hostile that she did not function as well as she might have. She appeared interested in the students, but her hostility towards me stood in the way of her overall teaching performance.

Another thing that interfered with the performance of these three teachers was their negative attitude towards the students. They did not put themselves into their work in such a way that would help the students. They adopted a "superior than thou" attitude, as if they were doing the students a favor by just being there. They did not put forth an effort to show even a semblance of really caring.

I submitted weekly reports to my Peace Corps Director, indicating to him the problems I was facing with the three volunteers. At first, he tried to evade this serious issue, mainly because he did not want to have an attrition rate on his record. He was more concerned with the numbers than with the education of the African students and the ultimate success of the school.

Finally, towards the end of March, 1975, after countless encounters and confrontations, the Peace Corps Director realized that the only solution would be to dismiss these volunteers, especially the commerce teacher and the typing teacher. These two teachers finally resigned from the secretarial school and returned to the United States. The shorthand teacher indicated that she wanted to remain at the school. Needless to say, her performance improved with the exit of the other two volunteers.

When the typing teacher left, I took on her job in addition to my other duties as principal and office practice teacher. Since the commerce teacher had also left, Madam Jane assumed the role of commerce teacher in addition to her English teaching and other assignments. We now had an enrollment of 57 students, three teachers, and a hell of a lot of work to do!

When our school first opened, I was astonished and discouraged to see the kinds of typewriters that were available for our classes. These typewriters, donated by the United States Peace Corps were deplorable! Some of them must have been 40 years old or more, with broken and missing parts. Others were beyond repair. Initially, the machines had actually been thrown in a heap in one of the classrooms. I cried when I saw the condition of the typewriters. When I voiced my concern to the Peace Corps staff, they told me that they had a Peace Corps volunteer who would take care of repairs and maintenance. As it turned out, there was a lack of spare parts for these machines in the country; also the fact that many of the machines were so old spare parts were practically non-existent.

I have learned during my travels that the United States, in its humanitarian efforts towards Third World countries, tends to donate the worse equipment and material available. Junk, just Junk, to say the least! I asked Peace Corps for replacements, but none ever came. I questioned why they ever considered giving this junk to the school. The cost of shipment alone would have paid for decent manual typewriters.

As an employee of AT&T Bell Laboratories, I decided to call upon my company for help with the typewriter situation. My previous assignment had been that of instructor and supervisor of secretarial studies. I decided to write to my former supervisor, Mrs. Mildred Boyd. I knew that Bell Laboratories often upgraded its typewriters and sometimes put the old ones in storage. They would later sell them or donate them, and usually they were in relatively good condition.

After many months of going through endless but necessary channels, Mildred Boyd wrote to me and informed me that she had managed to get Bell Laboratories to donate 12 IBM electric typewriters to our school! Freight and custom costs would be picked up by Bell Laboratories. I was ecstatic! What an overwhelming gesture of support from Bell Laboratories, and what a wonderful thing Mrs. Boyd was doing for us! Although these typewriters were electric, and the students were only use to manual machines, I felt that eventually they would be able to master these machines. I knew it would still take many months before the typewriters arrived, but just knowing that they were on the way took a load off my mind.

As we progressed in our training at the secretarial school, we were eventually able to bring in guest speakers. In early May, Messrs. Olson and Omondi came from the Ministry Of Commerce to address the students. We were also honored to have a visit from six Japanese dignitaries who were interested in the school and our progress. Gradually, we continued to have guest speakers from many areas of industry, all who played an important role in expanding our students' knowledge of the outside business world.

In mid-May, 1975, I was pleasantly surprised and delighted to receive visitors from the United States. Two employees of Bell Laboratories with whom I had previously worked, came to Kenya on safari holiday along with their husbands. Carol and Tony Rustako, and Sheila and Marvin Wiggins contacted me when they arrived. I met them in town at the Hilton Hotel where they were staying. They treated me to a sumptuous lunch while I related to them the trials and tribulations encountered at the school. Their visit really brought a ray of sunshine into my life!

1ST STUDENT ENROLLMENT NYSSS 1974

PURITY AND ESTHER

MADAM JANE WITH STUDENTS

CAROL RUSTAKO, RAINETTE, & SHEILA WIGGINS

School Curriculum

4

As previously mentioned, the curriculum at the secretarial school consisted of English, commerce, shorthand, typewriting, and office practice. This chapter summarizes these subjects..

English is one of the most important, if not the most important subject taught in Africa. As in the United States, students must show a definite mastery of the English language. Not just the spoken word itself, but all elements of English before being considered successful candidates for graduation from a secondary school. Punctuation, grammar, usage and spelling must be mastered. Writing skills must be attained. The student should also be proficient in reading comprehension and vocabulary skills.

I must emphasize the key role the English teacher, Jane Otto, played in teaching the

Kenyan women English. She used countless props, in addition to the local newspapers, English text, magazines, and special articles. I know, for a fact, that Madam Jane worked until the wee hours in the morning at home to prepare these young women for the English examinations. Were it not for her dedication and determination, our venture at the secretarial school would have failed. The students loved Madam Jane.

They could never have succeeded without her help, her kindness, and exceptionally skillful teaching. Not only was

Madam Jane a wonderful teacher, but her sincerity and communication with the students was overwhelming. As the students moved to each stage of the English examinations, the lessons became more difficult, but Madam Jane became more skillful and dedicated in her efforts to help these women of Kenya succeed.

The commerce course also plays a tremendously important part in the African student's education. It was the most difficult subject that the students had to overcome. There was a definite correlation between the English and commerce curriculum in that questions on the English examinations very often were related to commerce problems. Commerce covered areas such as production, standard of living, economics, money and banking, international trade, economic development of East Africa, and various phases of marketing. The effective teachings of Madam Jane's English classes proved to be most beneficial when the students sat for their commerce examinations.

The next subjects which were also of primary importance were typewriting and office practice. The object of Stage I Typewriting was to teach the student how to touch type at a minimum speed of 30 words per minute. This included a five-minute timed writing from straight copy material with a 2% or less error rate.

The next phase of typewriting was Stage II. Now the student has to increase the speed to 40-50 words per minute. Upon completion of a two-year typing course, the students were expected to have the skills and knowledge necessary to obtain a passing grade on the East African Examinations, Stage I and Stage II.

Here, I would like to elaborate a bit on the difference between typing courses in the United States and those in many African countries. In the United States, typing examinations usually consist of a 20-minute aptitude test and a five or ten-minute typing test. That's it. If you pass the aptitude test, you go on to the typing test, usually a simple 40-50 words per minute qualification test consisting of a few simple paragraphs. Pass these two tests and you are considered a qualified typist.

Well, not so with the African examinations! The first test consists of a ten-minute timing. Then you go on to problem solving, that is, four or five typing exercises. These exercises consist of editing, drafts to be finalized, business letters to be set up and corrected, and then a difficult tabulation exercise. The entire typing examination for Stage I is two hours. Stage II is even more difficult. In fact, the East African Examination Council examination is much more challenging and cannot even be equated with the less challenging tests administered in the United States, not just in the schools, but also in the corporate world. When the African student passes these examinations, she has made a tremendous achievement and can truly be rated as a qualified typist.

An additional teaching tool that I introduced to the students was the use of an automated system for teaching typing that I had brought with me from the United States. This system consisted of 13 cassette tapes, each tape progressively more difficult, until the student was able to master the tapes at 50 words per minute. The tapes were not used until the students had progressed favorably in the basic stages of typewriting. They were very useful and the students enjoyed using them. The tapes had a rhythmic tone to them, and the students actually exhibited a rhythmic motion when using them. I had used this system at Bell Laboratories when teaching my upward mobility program, and had found them to be extremely helpful. They worked at Bell Laboratories and they worked in East Africa with my rural students!

The next subject, office practice, tied in directly with the typing course. Office practice helped the students develop poise, self-confidence, and inter-personal skills necessary for secretarial employment. Telephone techniques, office procedures and countless office responsibilities were incorporated in the office practice course. Visual aids, such as telephone and interview training skits, films, charts, posters, magazines, the post office guide, and monthly field trips were instrumental in the successful completion of this course.

Now we come to another important subject, shorthand. The shorthand syllabus for the secretarial school took in the following objectives: First year, ability to take shorthand at speeds of 60-70 words per minute and be able to pass the E.A.E.C. Examination, Stage I. Second year, ability to take shorthand at speeds of 80-90 words per minute and be able to pass the E.A.E.C. Examination, Stage II.

The first efort in shorthand was the introduction of a system called Forkner shorthand. This was an abbreviated long hand system similar to speedwriting, another type of long hand that was used extensively in the United States. Both of these systems are designed to provide legible methods of writing, but at relatively low speeds. Speeds of up to 90-120 words per minute are seldom achieved. The Forkner method used a combination of longhand and symbols. Consequently, principles to be mastered were at a minimum.

The standard method of teaching shorthand in Europe has always been the Pitman method, which was introduced by Sir Issac Pitman, circa 1837. To date, it is still the most prevalent system in the English speaking world outside the United States.

The Pitman system was used in the United States for a long period of time. Around 1888, John Robert Gregg (Irish born) introduced the Gregg system of shorthand to England. However, it was not too successful there, Pitman being the more popular choice. In 1893, Gregg brought his system to the United States. The Pitman system was strongly entrenched in the eastern part of the country, so Gregg concentrated his introductory efforts in the Chicago area.

The Pitman method was extremely difficult and the time required to master the system was lengthy. As time evolved, however, many changes and improvements were made in the system to make it easier. The Gregg system, although it too was difficult, seemed to have a more effective audience in the United States. It was a good system with a good service and eventually became the predominant shorthand system in the United States. Both Pitman and Gregg systems evolved to the place where they had high speed potentials. Because of their basic phonetic structure, these two systems have been adopted successfully throughout the world.

The decision of the Washington Peace Corps office to introduce the Forkner shorthand system to the National Youth Service students, was, in my opinion, a gross mistake. The shorthand syllabus used at the secretarial school was the same as that used by all the private and government schools in Africa. Speeds of 60-120 words per minute were required on the various examinations, Stage I, II, and III, and Pitman system was being used. The art of good shorthand is closely associated with good writing and speaking as a tool for scholarly purposes. Forkner shorthand was definitely not the answer for our students. As with other combination long-hand and symbol methods, it slows down the student, rather than enabling the student to attain appreciable speeds.

Why Forkner? Again, as with the case of the broken down typewriters donated by Peace Corps, white America's concept of minorities not needing the best was clearly evidenced. After all, these African women were from rural areas. They could not possibly learn the difficult strokes of Pitman or Gregg shorthand.

Peace Corps administrators did not take into consideration the fact that Africans, after independence, had attended some of the same private and government schools that had once been offered only to the British ruling population. As was the case with the European students, the Africans were able to learn Pitman also. Some of these "free" Africans had backgrounds similar to our National Youth Service women, and they had been able to learn Pitman. Why bring in this mediocre, second-class system for our students at the secretarial school? Ironically, when I first applied for Peace Corps service a year before I was accepted, I was offered a position in Sierra Leone to teach Pitman shorthand. I was turned down because I was a Gregg shorthand teacher, and Washington, at that time, insisted on having a Pitman teacher.

I believe Peace Corps Washington clearly underestimated the capabilities and potential of the National Youth Service women when they elected to introduce the Forkner method in our school. Also, Peace Corps assigned a volunteer who was not even a qualified teacher, let alone qualified to teach Forkner, Gregg, or Pitman shorthand. She was, however, a white American, and in Peace Corps Washington's opinion, capable of teaching Africans. This same concept is often followed in the United States when it comes to teaching minorities. When the shorthand teacher completed her Peace Corps assignment, I took over the shorthand classes until a replacement was found. When I began teaching the students, it was clearly apparent that they had not mastered the Forkner method. The speeds were still at 60-70 words per minute, and they were extremely weak in reading and transcribing their outlines.

My only recourse was to give intense remedial instruction. Although the first group of students sat for Stage I Shorthand examinations, only a few passed. The Forkner method should never have been introduced and it was clearly a failure at the secretarial school.

I worked with the shorthand classes until another white American Peace Corps volunteer, Mrs. Robertson, arrived. She was a qualified teacher and had previously taught Pitman shorthand in Ghana, West Africa. Since she was experienced with the Pitman method, the Forkner system was discontinued and Pitman introduced. And, guess what? These poor, African women from the rural areas learned Pitman shorthand! Contrary to many American concepts, the African student, like any other student in the world, is capable of learning if taught by qualified, skilled, and concerned teachers. In fact, in many instances, the African students go on to excel in their various academic fields.

PRINCIPAL CHECKING TYPING PERFORMANCE

Hadithi 1-A Routine 48 Hours

5

During my Peace Corps assignment at the secretarial school, I encountered many setbacks, disappointments, and all kinds of frustrating experiences that one could never imagine. But looking back, I can also attach a bit of humor to some of these situations. From time to time, I will digress from my general narrative and give the reader a look into some of these events. I call these events "Hadithi," a Swahili word meaning story. I often refer to myself as "Princ" (short for principal) in these events. Take a trip with me as I relate Hadithi 1:

8:15 am: Scene—National Youth Service Secretarial School, (English Teacher, Madam Jane, approaching principal). "Madam, the students' choo (pronounced cho, meaning toilets) are filthy! The cleaning man couldn't possibly have cleaned them last night; or this morning either."

(Principal rings headquarters). She asks for the Commandant, Mr. Atteng, but he is away on leave. She asks for the Assistant Director, Mr. Ngumi, but he is away attending some kind of school. Finally, principal gets the training officer, Mr. Owitti. "Yes, principal. That is not my area, but I will take care of it for you this time. I will ring you back."

8:45 am: The choo cleaner comes running down to the school to see the principal. "Madam, I cleaned the toilets at 6:30 this morning! The students have dirtied them already." (Students usually arrive between 7:15 and 8:00 am). Principal follows choo cleaner to look at the toilets. (Principal musing to herself): Yes, they really are dirty, and the students are still using newspaper instead of the toilet paper. Some toilets are not flushed. Must tell Madam Jane to lecture to the students again during their personal hygiene class. I remember when we first opened, some of the students were standing on the toilet seats instead of sitting on them. Most of the students were used to standing or squatting when relieving themselves because this is the way the African toilets ae built in many of the bush and village areas. There is usually a large hole in the ground rather than a regular commode.

Principal then tells the choo cleaner that the matter will be taken care of. Choo cleaner also informs principal that toilet paper is running low. Principal checks. There are only seven rolls left; also need cleaning supplies for the toilets. Principal decides to ring supply stores right away. Stores area (called DARA Yard) is located in another part of town, about a 15-minute ride from the school.

10:00 am: Principal rings DARA Yard. She speaks to one of the workers. "Yes, Madam, I will check and have a box of toilet paper sent to the secretarial school this afternoon."

12:45 pm: Lunch time for all. Students go back to camp.

1:00 pm: Principal and teachers eating and resting in lounge. All is serene.

2:00 pm: Students return to classes. Classes only 55 minutes today, instead of one hour and twenty minutes. This is Sports Day at school. Sports begin at 3:15 pm.

2:55 pm: Principal and Madam Jane rush students to change clothes for soccer. Shorthand teacher rushes students to change for volley ball. Meanwhile, Judo students are waiting for 3:00 o'clock bus to DARA Yard. These students go for Judo lessons on Sports Day.

3:00 pm: Bus is usually here by 2:30, waiting for the students. Better ring Mr. Owitti again and find out what's happening. "Yes, principal. This is not my area. Besides three buses went to Mombasa today. There is only one left. I don't think you will get a bus today. I will check and ring you back."

3:15 pm: Principal and Madam Jane go out on sports field and participate in warm-up exercises with soccer team, coached by Mr. Ochi Nakamara, Japanese volunteer. Principal and Madam Jane run around field for a little exercise.

One of the students calls the principal: "Madam, you are wanted on the simu (telephone). It is Mr. Owitti's office. Madam, here is DARA Yard." (A lady is on the telephone this time). "Madam, do you still want a bus?"

"Yes, I want a bus."

"It is coming."

Principal returns to sports field. She informs Judo students that bus is coming. Ochi Nakamura approaches the principal. "Principal, there is only one football. I need many, at least four."

"I know, Ochi. I told Mr. Githaiga, but he says, "hakuna pesa." (there is no money).

Nakamura says, "But I saw Mr. Salamba (sports counterpart for Ochi) buying balls yesterday. Please ring him." Principal goes and rings Mr. Salamba. There is no answer.

3:25 pm: Bus still not here and sports are over at 4:15 pm. Principal and Madam Jane sit on grass with Judo students and watch soccer practice.

4:00 pm: The bus is here! It's too late, but Judo team wants to go anyway. "All right, says principal. Go ahead. Kwaherini."

4:15 pm: Time to leave. NYS bus is here to take staff to town, along with administrative personnel from headquarters, about 30 people. (When I first started traveling to school, I had to take a public bus from town; however, NYS finally made arrangements for school staff to be picked up with regular NYS personnel. This made things a bit easier for me). Principal suddenly remembers, "Darn it! That toilet paper never did arrive."

5:00 pm: NYS bus drops principal off at Tusker building where she catches her second bus. Other teachers live within walking distance in town. Principal, thinking as she waits for bus: I hope the #18 bus gets here first tonight and is not too crowded. #18 puts me close to home, but #23 means a two-mile walk home.

5:30 pm: Ah, here's #18, and not bad! Only a few people to knock the ole princ about before she climbs on the bus. Standing room, but they're not like sardines tonight; not yet anyway. Still a few more stops to make. Ah, finally, a seat! Just happened to be standing beside the right person at the right time. It's in the back, but it's a seat!

6:30 pm: (Bus approaching the principal's stop). Only one more mile to go. Principal gets up. It's time to start worming her way towards the front of the bus. You can't get off from the back. It's not allowed. Besides, people coming in from the back will crush you. Ah, the principal finally makes it to the front. Only about 40 people to slide by. She's off!

(Principal to herself again). Will stop at supermarket and buy a bottle of beer to go with dinner. Eureka! They have sukari (sugar) today! Haven't been able to find any on the shelves for more than a week. Will get two bags; one for home, one for school.

6:15 pm: Home at last! Exhausted! Glad I cooked last night for tonight's meal. Cabbage, smoked belly, plus a bottle of beer. Smoked belly same as slab bacon back home, only more than just a "streak of lean" over here in Kenya.

7:15 pm: Really should do some studying tonight, or write some letters, but I'm too tired. Maybe tomorrow.

8:00 pm: And so to bed.

6:30 am: Must hurry! Just have time for cup of chai and maziwa (tea with milk) and slice of mkate (bread). Old fashion "depression" breakfast back in the states. (Have it every morning over here).

7:15 am   (Principal leaves house to catch #18 bus, and as usual musing to herself) Here comes #18. Uh-Oh! They're hanging out the door again! Oh well, will have to try and get it anyway. Everyone else does. Pole! Pole! (sorry, sorry). I can't make it. It's just too crowded! Wait, here comes another #18. Standing room only, but room! Princ is on! Conductor steadily chanting, "Songea mbele! Songea mbele!" (Move up front!) How the hell can you move up front when there are 40 or 50 people in front of you! Besides, if anyone moves up front, someone will fall out the door! Hope I get to town before NYS bus leaves the Tusker building.

8:05 am: In town, but too late. NYS bus has just pulled off. Princ will have to dodge buses, cars, push carts, and trot around to Public Bus Station. About a five-minute trot. #5 or #5A leaves at 8:15. Still have time to make it.

8:20 am: Here comes #5, and plenty of room! Only this ride costs 80 shillings (15 cents U.S. money). NYS bus is free. Better check out the bus driver. Hope it's not the muslim. Had him last week. He took those curves at 90 miles an hour. Old princ and lady sitting next to her had to hold on for dear life, as he rounded each bend, to keep from sliding on the floor. The driver looks OK. He has on a cowboy hat though. Hope he doesn't drive like one.

Here's the bus stop. One minute to get to class. I see someone has put the coffee on. Good! Will double back later and have a cup.

8:30 am: "Hamjambo."

"Hatujambo, Madam."

"Ladies, this morning we will try typing tape #6. After that a five-minute timing; then another tape which will be explained to you later." (Principal puts tape on).

8:40 am: Lights go out! Tape goes off!

"Oh well ladies, let's do some warm-ups until the power comes back on."

(Principal notices two men approaching classroom. I wonder what they want?)

"Excuse me, Madam. We are from the Ministry of Works. Your power is off."

"Yes, I know."

"Didn't anyone tell you?"

"No, they didn't."

Men tell principal that power will be off for rest of the day.

"Ladies, we will continue with warm-ups, and then a five-minute timing. After that, dictation and transcribing to the typewriter."

9:30 am: Chai and/or Kahawa break. (Good thing coffee had finished perking before the power went off. A bit lukewarm, but better than nothing). Darn! I'll have to go to DARA Yard and get that toilet paper. Will have to dial Stores. No luck. Telly out of order. Guess here in Kenya when the power goes off, the telly goes off.

12:45 pm: Lunch time and telly is still out. Toilet paper going fast.

2:00 pm: Classes resume. There's John, the security guard, outside. Brings me letter from my niece, Kim. I will have John walk to headquarters and tell Mr. Owitti that I need transport to DARA Yard.

2:45 pm: Here comes John back. "Madam, Mr. Owitti has left. The commandant is not here. Mrs. Amoeba has left. General China has left. There is no one."

"Well, please go tell Mr. Githaiga that the principal needs transport to DARA Yard because the toilet paper is finished."

"Yes, Madam, I will go now."

3:30 pm: Here comes John again and he's in the GK-1! (Mr. Githaiga's chauffeur driven car). Chauffeur Njiru is here to transport principal to DARA Yard. Principal hops in vehicle, and she and John take off with Njiru. "Oh, wait a minute. Stop! I must tell Madam Jane to dismiss typing class at 3:55. OK, let's go."

3:45 pm: At DARA Yard. Principal orders toilet paper, soap, and rags for cleaning. "Any Kiwi?" (for cleaning toilet bowls).

"It is finished."

"Any Vim?"

"It is finished."

"Oh well, hurry with the toilet paper, please. I have to be back in time to catch the 4:30 bus to town."

"Yes, Madam, but you will have to sign this indent. Take it over to the office and get a signature."

Principal trots over to office to get signature from one of the clerks; then trots back to Stores office. Princ looks around. Toilet paper is not in sight.

Aha! That young man "working" over there is rising to his feet. Slowly, but surely, he saunters over by the steps and grabs some towel rags; then saunters over to another spot. There's the toilet paper! And there are ten cakes of lifebuoy soap!

Principal stands patiently waiting. The young man is coming her way. In just a few minutes he will hand the supplies over. Principal signs indent. There, done!

"Put the toilet paper in the trunk, John. Let's go Njiru. Thank you, thank you, sir. Kwaheri."

4:10 pm: We're almost there. Here's the school at last! What's this? The gate is closed! John jumps out of car to open the gate. OK. Students have left. It's now 4:25.

4:28 pm: "Put the toilet paper in the reception area for now, John. Rags and soap over there. OK ladies, let's make it before the bus leaves us."

Principal notices someone up ahead on a motorcycle. (What does he want? Oh, he has mail).

Motorcycle driver shouts to principal, "Madam, it is for you."

"Well, I'll be dog-gone. It's a package notice from Mr. & Mrs. John Dickerson (my sister and brother-in-law). Hurray!"

(Principal musing on bus). Let's see, when did Betty say she sent the packages? November? This is May. Six months ago. Oh, well, this is Kenya!

I'll have to wait until Saturday to pick up the packages. Must get some shillings from the bank first. Don't know what the duty charges will be. Two packages? Well, it wasn't such a bad day after all. Gifts from home! Mzuri sana!

Let's see. I will have to take #18 tonight and get closer to home. Can stop at supermarket for a bottle of beer; but then, if #23 comes along, can stop at Westlands shopping center and get a bottle of wine, only that means a two-mile walk home. Really should celebrate Betty and Johnny's packages with a bottle of wine; but gee, beer is only two shillings and wine is 19 shillings. That's a lot of shillings. Only have 25 shillings until tomorrow when I go to the bank. Oh well, we'll see. Whichever bus comes first. #18, the beer; #23, the wine.

Here's the Princ at the Tusker building again, waiting for the right bus to come along. Looks like #17 coming. No, that's the #8 bus to Kibera. What's this coming? No, that's the #7 to Kenyatta hospital. Uh-oh, what's this? It's #23, and it's practically empty! Well, guess the princ will be going to Westlands!

Changes

6

When I arrived at the secretarial school the following Monday, I received great news! The National Youth Service had obtained a commerce teacher for the school. A male Kenyan by the name of Simon Peter Mburu, a prophetic name to say the least! He had come to relieve us of some of our burdens. Now, Madam Jane would be able to devote full time to her English classes.

The arrival of Mr. Mburu was indeed a blessing. He was well qualified, having previously taught at one of the other government institutions. Also, the fact that he was Kenyan made his coming to us more significant. He was able to relate to the students, and they, in turn were able to interact with him. He had a wealth of knowledge about his country and was able to impart this information to the students. He was a family man with a wife and seven children. When not in the classroom, he devoted much of his time helping to raise his wonderful family.

Simon, as I learned to call him as we became better acquainted, was indeed like an ambassador to me. He often took the time to relate meaningful and historical facts about Kenya. Also, when we went on class field trips, his expertise about commercial business within the country was enlightening and educational. Simon was, indeed, personable and very effective. He was extremely dependable, and as we progressed at the school, he became my "second right hand!"

In retrospect, I realize now that many of the trials and tribulations we experienced at the school could have been avoided if only Peace Corps, Washington, had done its homework. The combination of initially unqualified, incompetent teachers, poor equipment, and mediocre teaching systems greatly hampered our first efforts at the school. Fortunately, in the long run, with the addition of Mr. Mburu to our staff, we were able to overcome many obstacles.

A few months after Mr. Mburu arrived, another Kenyan teacher, Mr. Ngugi, joined our staff. He assisted Mr. Mburu with the commerce classes and also proved to be instrumental in the success of our teaching efforts.

Later, when I completed my assignment as principal of the secretarial school, Mr. Mburu was appointed by the Director of the National Youth Service to take over my position. This proved to be a wise choice, as Mr. Mburu demonstrated competence and professionalism the entire time he served as principal. While he was principal of the secretarial school, Simon pursued his education further and eventually earned a degree in Adult Education.

When I first moved into my cottage in Westlands, I was fortunate enough to obtain the services of my landlord's servant, Alphonse. Having a servant in Africa does not constitute wealth, since the servants are paid very small wages. When I say small, I mean an average of two or three dollars per week. In my case, it was a means of economically helping an African to compensate for the low wages he was receiving. As Peace Corps volunteers we were encouraged by the staff to hire servants when possible, even if it only meant just having someone do our laundry or minor chores.

Alphonse was a quiet, family man. Like many of the men in Kenya, he had a large family living back in one of the rural villages. He had come to Nairobi to work in order to feed his family. Under these conditions he was only able to spend a few months with his family, usually during various Christian holidays. While he was with me, I made it a point never to treat Alphonse as a servant, but as a friend. I tried to get him to sit at my kitchen table and eat with me, however, I sensed his embarrassment at this so I did not insist. Nevertheless, we always maintained a pleasant relationship during the time he worked for me.

The male servants, in most cases, are not permitted to bring their families with them to the town where they are working. Their living quarters are very small and sparsely furnished. I would even venture to say that some of the living quarters were totally unfit to live in, even for one person. Most of the servants were employed by Europeans or other foreigners, and these employers did not extend themselves to provide suitable quarters for their African servants and their families.

The wives of the male servants remained in the villages, taking care of their children and tending their crops. Although very poor, the African family always had enough land to raise their own vegetables and fruits. Their crops also served as a means of income. One would often see the women from the villages, trudging along the road, selling their home-grown crops. Sometimes they had a huge bag atop their heads, filled with maize, sukuma wiki, or some other produce, plus a baby strapped to their backs and a few more watoto (children) trailing along.

Part of my adjusting to various things in Africa, concerns an event that occurred while I was living in my first residence, the cottage. One evening when the rainy season began, I came home from school only to be greeted by a swarm of flying insects outside my door. When I entered my cottage, there were hundreds of them flying all over the place! I swatted and swatted with a newspaper, and they went down quickly, but they were still oncoming! I could not control them! Finally, really upset and terrified, I ran out of the cottage to my landlord's house. His wife assured me that they were harmless termites. During the rainy season, which is also mating time, they come out in droves.

The landlord's wife gave me a yellow bulb to put in my outdoor overhead socket. She informed me that this would keep the termites from swarming around the house. I returned to my cottage and met a room full of dead termites. Seemingly, they only live for a short time, and my swatting caused them to drop dead almost instantly. I later learned that these termites are often saved, dried out, and used as a source of food.

In early August, more changes occurred. A new Peace Corps volunteer arrived to take over the typewriting and office practice courses! Beverly Dretzke came to our school with excellent credentials. She was a qualified teacher, efficient, and well-trained in her field. I continued teaching typing to the original group of students, preparing them for their E.A.E.C. examinations. After they completed Stage I, I continued working with these students, to help them prepare for advance typewriting, Stage II.

Madam Beverly worked with the new group of students who had recently enrolled at the secretarial school. She also took complete charge of the office practice classes. Perhaps it was a bit symbolic that Madam Beverly arrived in August 1975, marking a year that I had been serving as a volunteer in Kenya, and what a year it had been! Getting her certainly took some of the pressure off of me.

In September, we were pleasantly surprised and happy to receive ten used manual typewriters from the National Youth Service. Although used, they were in very good condition. My efforts in pleading for help from headquarters had not been in vain. Finally, could this mean that the male officials were beginning to realize that our "girls" were making progress?

In late September, I received more good news. Another Peace Corps volunteer, was completing her two-year stint and would be leaving

Kenya. She had been living in a very nice duplex-type apartment. The building was leased by Peace Corps to house some of its volunteers. I was informed that I could have the apartment. It was spacious and comfortable, two bedrooms, living-dining area, a small but compact kitchen, and completely furnished. Also, it was still in the area close to where I had my cottage. Transportation was even more convenient, since I only had to walk a short distance to catch the #18 bus to town.

I was ecstatic! Since the apartment had been previously furnished by Peace Corps, whenever a new volunteer moved in, the furniture remained. I only had to bring my limited supply of household goods and clothing.

My neighbors were a friendly Luo family. They included a doctor of education who taught at the University of Nairobi, his wife, also a teacher at one of the elementary schools, and their two young children. I even had a front porch and beautiful surrounding shrubbery.

I soon settled comfortably in my new quarters and became quite friendly with my neighbors. Within a few months, I had what I thought was a rather unusual experience. The mother of my neighbor (the Luo wife) paid a visit to their home to attend her grandson's birthday party. Imagine my surprise when my neighbor asked me to take her mother in as an overnight guest. Seemingly, it is the custom in some African families that the mother-in-law is not permitted to stay under the same roof with her daughter and husband once they are African families that the are married. It is considered to be unethical to be in their presence in case they engage in marital relations, and the mother might overhear them.

Not knowing about this custom at the time, I thought it strange that the request had been made; however, I took the mother in. When the mother came over that evening, she brought her own bed linen (this too was an African custom), and I welcomed her.

In Africa, the mother-in-law does not "pop in" just anytime for a visit. She has to be formally invited at all times. Also, at the grandson's birthday party, she stayed in the kitchen until her son-in-law asked her to join the guests. This is quite a difference from our western culture and our mother-in-law customs.

Alphonse followed me to my new residence. However, he soon took another evening position in addition to the regular job he had with my former landlord. Consequently, I had to get another servant. Alphonse recommended a friend of his, David, and he began working for me as soon as Alphonse left. During the rest of my stay in Kenya, David worked out fine.

SIMON WITH HIS FAMILY OF SEVEN CHILDREN

MADAM BEVERLY WITH
SECRETARIAL STUDENTS

Hadithi 2
Happenings With The
Principal

7

26 May 1975. Up at 6:30 am. Regular depression breakfast. Caught #18 nearby. Almost in town; #18 bus packed and jammed, as usual. Bus has trouble making it up Museum Hill. Conductor finally tells passengers to get off and help push bus up the hill. Many of the passengers help, but ole princ just stands by and watches. Another bus is approaching, and then all the passengers leave the crippled bus and run towards the second one. They're scrambling and pushing, trying to get on the other bus! Principal decides, "hapana" (no). Meanwhile conductor, left alone now, is still trying to make it up the hill. Finally gets over! Some of the passengers, including the principal, hop back on the first bus. We're off again!

Arrive at Tusker too late for NYS bus. Must take #5A from public bus station. Just have time. Ah! There's #5A, and everybody rushes towards it. What's this? Bus driver suddenly changes number of bus to #2 (this happens often). Oh well, maybe the next one in will be #5A. Here it is, finally. Might be a little late for school this morning.

It's already 8:40 am. Ten minutes late, but I'm here! Must hurry to typing class.

As soon as principal reaches classroom, she sees Mrs. Omitti, servicewoman officer, approaching the school. Principal thinks to herself, Rebecca (Mrs. Omitti) must want something. She never comes down here like she should unless she wants the students for something. I wonder what's happening now?

"Good morning, principal."

"Good morning, Rebecca."

(Rebecca takes seat in staff room). "Principal, Sgt. Muthoni (one of the students) is out sick today."

"Yes, I know, Rebecca. Last week Sgt. Muturi (another student officer) informed me that Sgt. Muthoni is pregnant. Also, Moinda (another student). Is that correct?"

"Well, principal, Sgt. Muthoni aborted over the week-end. In the camp. She took something Friday night and the baby came early Saturday morning. When I arrived, the baby was already there. Kidogo, kidogo (very small). I cut the cord. Then some people from the camp took Sgt. Muthoni to the hospital. The baby too."

"Well, Rebecca, what next? Does the director know?"

"No, principal, but everyone else in the camp knows."

"I won't say anything to the other teachers. It would only cause too much conversation. I didn't know Sgt. Muthoni was so far. She certainly concealed it. Was she not examined periodically like the other students?"

"She is the sergeant, principal. She was busy lining up the other students for their examinations, and no one thought to examine the sergeant."

"Oh, well, Rebecca, anything else?"

Rebecca hands principal small card with name of another student on it, Nyambura. She's pregnant too!

"Oh no, Rebecca, I was only kidding! Nyambura tried to get a pass from me this morning. She was wanted at home. I told her to see you."

"Yes, I know, principal. She just found out this morning that she is pregnant; that is we found out after she was examined. I fear she wants to leave the camp and go into town and get something to abort. I will not give her permission to leave."

"All right, Rebecca. I must get back to class."

Principal returns to her classroom, a bit pensive, but resigned to the report of the pregnancies. (Musing again) Let's see, that's four pregnant who have already left school; then two new ones, and now another one. Seven out of the original group, not counting four abortions that took place a few months ago. That makes 11 known pregnancies. Wow! Students may not be No. 1 in the classroom, but they certainly are prolific!

12:45 pm: Lunch time. Students return to camp.

2:00 pm: Back to classes. One more after this. Then the day is finally over!

3:00 pm: Receptionist, one of the secretarial students, comes to the classroom and informs principal that she is wanted by Mr. Atteng, NYS Commandant. Principal goes to her office and greets Mr. Atteng.

"Habari, Mr. Atteng."

"Habari, Madam." (Principal is suspicious when commandant visits. It usually means that the students are going some place which will interrupt their regular classes.

"Madam, as you know, we are getting ready for Madaraka Day here in Kenya. Sunday, June 1st, the students will have to parade before the president."

"Yes, Mr. Atteng, I know. They have been practicing every evening after school."

"Yes, but you see, Madam, they have to be smart and right for the president. Beginning tomorrow, I will have the students every day, starting at noon and then all day on Friday. That is, if it's all right with you, Madam."

"Hapana! Hapana! (No! No!) I was to be given advance notice, like two or three days, if the students have to leave the school before Friday. Hapana! Hapana!

"All right, Madam, not tomorrow then, say kesho kutwa (day after tomorrow). You can have them from 28th, 29th noon, and all day Friday."

"All right. I guess there's nothing we can do about it, but are you sure you won't be taking them tomorrow, too?"

"No, Madam. Hapana. Only what we have agreed upon now, unless there are unusual circumstances, but I will ring you first if there is a change. Thank you, Madam. Kwaheri.

"Kwaheri, Mr. Atteng." (Principal returns to classroom)

4:30 pm: Principal and other teachers leave for town.

5:00 pm: Principal arrives in town. She decides to walk to main post office and mail important letter to Bell Laboratories regarding the typewriters. On way to post office, principal notices that traffic seems to be a bit heavier than usual. Wonder what's going on? Principal decides to walk towards University Way and catch #18 bus from there.

Principal notices that people seem to be gathered in small groups along the way. Something's buzzing! Broken glass in middle of the street. Must have been an auto accident. Principal arrives at bus stop. University is directly across the street.

Uh-oh! What's this? Looks like the GSU (government police). Hundreds of them! They're surrounding the university. What's going on?

Young Asian, standing next to the principal, says, "The students are acting up again. It's been going on all day."

From time to time, on various occasions, university students rebel against the government or university staff. Principal looks around. Only a few people waiting here for the bus. Wonder if I should stand here. Rather close to the university. Just then, a few of the GSU officers turn around and look towards the area where the principal is standing.

"Get away! Get away! Get the bus at the next corner! Move away from there! Move away!"

Principal and five or six others scurry along, making it to the next corner, about a block away.

At corner now, principal and others pause and look towards the university. GSU are lined up all the way. What's this? Students, about fifty of them, on top of the university roof! Hands raised! They're surrendering to the police! Small crowd of young people gather near the principal, and start murmuring a bit. New batch of GSU police turn and look across at the crowd. Oops! They're coming this way, with rifles, shields, and billets! They're chasing the young crowd down the street! Right pass the principal, who by this time, has eased over to a nearby store entrance. There they go! Guess princ had better move on to another corner. Maybe bus stops here. Principal has now walked three blocks. Still no bus stop. Wait! Here comes #19, but it's not stopping. Where can I catch the next bus? Princ walks on. Lmost to the highway now. Ah! The red light has caught #18. Princ and a few more people run towards bus. We make it! Whew!

People are buzzing. As we ride along, we can see hundreds of police lined up all along the highway. Must have been something else here in town today! Glad to be living out near the country side. Just get me home, driver! I don't mind the packed bus today!

* *

Next day: Upon arising, Principal, musing as usual. Well, wonder what today will be like? Hope the university students have quieted down. Princ still "shook up" from yesterday's events.

7:15 am: Principal reading paper at bus stop. It is full of the university disturbance of yesterday. Guess I'll send clippings to the folks back home. Here comes #18, early today. Will be able to catch NYS bus if we don't get stuck on that hill again. Princ arrives at Tusker building NYS bus is waiting. Other teachers and staff already on the bus. Princ fills them in on yesterday's happenings at the university.

8:30 am: Princ arrives at school. Hope everything is peaceful today, and classes go according to schedule.

12:45 pm: Students leave for lunch.

2:00 pm: Students are back from lunch, and everything is fine.

2:10 pm: Uh-oh! Here comes Rebecca again, and she's in a hurry!

"Principal, principal, the students have to leave for practice! They are wanted right now!"

"But Rebecca, Mr. Atteng told me that they wouldn't be leaving in the afternoon until tomorrow!"

"I know, Madam, but he doesn't know what he's talking about. Today is a very important practice day. The band is here. They have to practice with the band. They are wanted now!"

"All right, Rebecca." Principal sticks her head in all the classrooms, telling the teachers, "We have to let them go, ladies. They are wanted back at camp, now! Let's go!" (Oh, well, another broken promise by Mr. Atteng; another early closing).

2:45 pm: Principal and teachers walking from school. Maybe NYS bus will come along and give us a lift. Regular bus doesn't leave until 4:30. Wait! Here comes an open truck. He's stopping! Principal greets them. "We need a lift to town. We'll ride in the back of the truck."

"No, no principal. You can ride in the front. We'll get in the back." Principal and other teachers squeeze up front with the driver, and we're off to town!

Principal and others arrive in town. Principal decides to stop and have ice cream and coffee with Madam Jane. Then on to her bus stop, away from the university, of course.

Principal stops in Westlands; does a little light shopping. Checks mail box. No mail from Sis or Kim. Well, maybe tomorrow. It's starting to rain. Princ will have to splurge (about 90 cents) and take a taxi. What a day!

Hadithi 3
Madaraka Day

8

This Holiday Is Celebrated Every Year To Commemorate

Kenya's Self-Rule And Responsibilities

After Independence

6:30 am: Up early this morning. Had good breakfast—nyama ya nguruwe, mayai, kahawa, mkate (meat, eggs, coffee, bread). Must hurry. Meeting Madam Jane at post office at 8:45. From there we will go to Uhuru Park for Madaraka Day celebration.

8:45 am: Running late. Heavy downpour. Will have to wait a while before making it to the bus stop. Bet the sun will come out by the time the president arrives. The way his luck is running (releasing all those students after the disturbance the other day) sure put him in good with the public. Certainly eased the tension that's been here for the past few days.

Hope everything goes all right today. Looking forward to the parade. Wish those airplanes wouldn't fly so low though. Saw one in October (Kenyatta Day) and thought it was going to crash. Really frightening. Oh well, guess it's part of the thrill of the ceremonies.

9:00 am: Principal boards #18. Not too crowded. It's Sunday morning. Guess bulk of crowd will be going to town later, after church.

9:15 am: There's Jane, patiently waiting. We stop at Intercontinental Hotel to use the Choo, then on to Uhuru Park. See some of the students who will be marching today. They greet us warmly with a vigorous handshake, as is the custom in Kenya. Jane and principal then move on to seating area. It's about 100 yards from where the president will be sitting, almost in front of him.

10:15 am: Park is beginning to fill up now. Dignitaries are beginning to arrive. There's the British High Commission representative, Lord Duff, arriving in his huge Rolls Royce. There's the French ambassador and the Italian ambassador. Also, a representative from Japan, a representative from the United States, and other dignitaries. Oh, here comes Margaret, the mayor, who also happens to be the president's daughter. Guess the president will be coming soon.

11:10 am: President is late. He was due here at 10:50 am. Traffic must be heavy.

11:15 am: Ah! Here comes the motorcade now. Lone, black dude approaching on motorcycle, smartly dressed. Here comes another one, as sharp as the first. Now here come about 30 more. Motorcycles are purring softly, not roaring. Now they break slowly, still in formation. The center is open. Here comes the president's escort car, down the middle, gliding through with about ten, big, black bodyguards packed in the Mercedes limousine. Now, here comes the president, directly behind them. He's riding in an open top Mercedes. President is standing, waving to the crowd with his "cow whisk," (a swishy cow's tail) that he always carries and waves during public appearances.

President's car pulls up. Out steps Mama Ngina (president's 4th wife, who is the one in office with him now). She's black and beautiful, about 39 years old, wearing a long, blue, flowing gown, blue headwrap, and mink stole draped around her shoulders.

Here comes Mzee (the president) stepping out on the other side, using a cane. He's 84 years old, but "standing tall" as he mounts the red-carpeted steps to the dais. The crowd is applauding loudly! Now the big parade can start!

11:30 am: Here they come, marching smartly! The 5th battalion, color guard, 1st platoon, parachutists, Air Force, Navy, policemen and policewomen, police dogs, horses, prison servicemen. They're great! Fabulous! Hundreds of them, and they are all black! Now here comes our National Youth Service students! My they look "smart." There's Rebecca, heading the group, eyes right, and saluting Mzee smartly!

The parade is almost over now. The traditional dancers come next. They're supposed to be really great! Oh, no, that's right, the president is standing now. I almost forgot. Those darn airplanes have to come by first and salute the president with a "flip over." Now everyone has to stand. This is the part the principal dreads. Be cool, princ. It's all part of the show.

12:10 pm: Here they come! Flying high the first time. They go around overhead, circle the tower, which is the tallest building in Nairobi. Princ nudges Jane, "Well, they made it without hitting the tower." Here they come again, lower this time. They make a complete flip over, right in front of the president. Here comes the #1 plane, swooping down, then a flip. Now here comes #1. He's even lower. Then a flip. He ascends, glides away. Now #3, same show, but each time flying lower. This is agonizing! If only they wouldn't fly so low! Princ hates these flybys.

Here comes #4. Lower, and lower, then a flip! He makes it and climbs on up, up and away!

The crowd is roaring and applauding as each pilot does his flip directly in front of the president. Meanwhile Princ is cringing and moaning as each plane goes by. Well, only one more to go, thank goodness!

Here comes the last plane. "Wow!" He's even lower! They shouldn't do this. Look at all those children up there, overhead, near the principal and Jane. Here he comes again. Oh, so low! Pilot does his flip, and now descends even lower! Uh-oh! He's not going to make it! He's coming down near those trees! Princ thinks she sees a red spark, or is it the tail light? He's too low! He can't make it back up! Princ hears Jane murmuring in the background, "Oh, he's going to crash!" Princ turns her head for a second to make sure no more planes are coming. Princ turns back quickly! The plane is going down! SWOOSH! A huge red ball of fire shoots up towards the sky! The crowd groans! Then, nothing. Just a faint wisp of smoke! Now, silence. Some people run toward the scene. It's a bit more than a kilometer away, but it looks even closer.

Princ sort of moves around in a daze. Jane is also shook up. We want to leave, but know that any sudden dash by anyone will cause pandemonium. Most of the crowd seems to sense this, and, finally, we all sit down, stunned!

Here come the traditional dances now (as if nothing had happened). Guess the "show must go on" (as we say back home). There are many different tribes. Can't really appreciate them now. Princ had really been looking forward to this part. The dancers continue on, boom-de-boom! Drums are beating, dancers are leaping high and singing, their hips shaking wildly! Each dancer is doing his/her "own thing" as they get in front of the presidents. It's not a long performance, but to the Princ it seems like ages!

12:45 pm: Now comes the president's speech. (Hope it isn't one of his very long ones). Officials are still moving about, sending messages through and to the president. Guess it's about the airplane crash. Mzee finally rises to his feet. He then asks for two minutes of silence for the "pilots ndega wawili." (The two pilots who were in the plane that crashed).

President then begins his speech, 20 minutes in English, then an "off-the-cuff" real speech to his people in Kiswahili. (Princ caught about two words.

2:00 pm: Well, it's finally over. Now for the battle out of this crowd. Not too bad. Guess everyone is so quiet and orderly due to the airplane tragedy. Princ walks on with Jane. Jane lives near Uhuru Park. She has invited Princ to have lunch with her and Jim (Jane's husband). What a delicious lunch! Big, fat, juicy beef burgers, French fries, onions, salad, and beer! We spent most of the time talking about the airplane crash. Jim said that some people saw it on television (yes, a few people do have TV here in Kenya).

4:00 pm: Princ leaves Jane and Jim, and heads for home. Gets dark around 6:00, so Princ has to leave now. By the time she makes bus connections and arrives home it will be almost 6 o'clock. It's about a mile walk from Jane's house to bus stop. Will catch bus along University Way (no problem today). Prince catches #23 home. She feels like walking another two miles today. That airplane crash was really disturbing.

Glad tomorrow is a holiday. Madaraka Day falling on a Sunday this year gives employees national holiday on Monday. Everything is closed. Will catch up on lesson plans tomorrow. Princ doesn't feel like it today. An exciting day, but a bit upsetting. Don't think Princ can sit through another flyby. Oh well, this is Kenya!

Family Addition

9

On September 21, 1975, a new ray of sunshine came into my life! As previously mentioned, during the course of my assignment at the secretarial school, I became very friendly with our Peace Corps consultant, Dr. Cynthia Perry, and her husband, Dr. James Perry. They "took me under their wing," so to speak and I frequently found myself spending the week-ends at their home, especially during lunch and dinner time. Their home was only a short distance from mine. I also enjoyed their three children, Paula, James, and Mark.

Well, this momentous day in September came, and the Perry's Siamese cat gave birth to five beautiful kittens. These kittens were supposedly sired by the male Siamese cat, also a member of the Perry household. But, lo and behold, when the litter arrived, it consisted of two white kittens (a common trait of the Siamese cat at birth) and three jet black kittens (not a common trait). We concluded that, somewhere along the way, Mama Siamese had also been dating an African cat who was not Siamese.

In any case, the kittens were beautiful. Dr. Perry eventually gave all the kittens away, including Mama and Papa. I was the happy recipient of one of the white kittens. At the age of four months, she became part of my household. When she began tearing my curtains on a daily basis, I decided to name her "Ripper."

Ripper was with me during my entire stay in Kenya. In fact, later on she gave birth to four kittens of her own. I gave two of them away and kept the other two. When I returned to the states after completion of my assignment, I brought Ripper and the two kittens back with me. I gave the two away, but Ripper stayed with me until she passed away at the age of 17.

Here, I would like to digress a bit and relate a brief incident that I encountered while traveling back and forth by bus to and from school. If nothing else, it taught me a lesson about how to be more careful

One day, after classes were over, I decided to go into the city of Nairobi and do a little shopping. When I completed my shopping I caught the #23 bus near the Hilton Hotel. I only had a few shillings remaining. As was my habit, I took out a ten-shilling note and put it in my jacket pocket while waiting for the bus. I often did this to avoid having to rummage through my purse for the bus fare in the presence of the crowd. Skillful pickpockets were rampant in the city of Nairobi.

As the bus approached, I noticed a young man yelling at the other end of the bus. I automatically turned my head to see what he was yelling about, but could not really understand him. By now, the bus door had opened and I pushed my way towards the entrance. When I reached in my pocket for my ten shillings, I discovered that the shillings were gone!

I alighted from the bus slowly, confused and dismayed, trying to regroup. I only had a few shillings left, just enough to catch another bus to Westlands. Now I would have to walk the rest of the way home, about three miles.

I started going over the events that had just taken place, and then began to realize that I had been "ripped off." The young man who had been yelling at the far end of the bus did this to distract me. When I turned towards him, another man working with him quickly put his hands in my pocket and took the ten shillings. This was a common trick in the city, and I had fallen for it! One interesting fact that I also noticed while in Africa. Even though the color of my skin was similar to that of many Africans, the African could always spot a black American. In this case, I was the "patsy." Here I was thinking that, after a year in Africa, I was a welcome "sister." Well, I learned my lesson, and consequently, took more precautions after this incident.

I finally took the next bus to Westlands, got off, and made the long journey by foot with empty pockets. I was tired, a bit disillusioned, but also a lot wiser.

RIPPER–SEPT. 21, 1975-FEB. 24, 1993

Examination Time

10

So-called "mock" examinations are held first, to prepare the students for the final East African examinations. The term mock is just what it means, an act of imitation. Sample tests are given to the students, and we, the teachers, act as invigilators. The tests are taken from actual examinations that had been given in previous years. We tried to make the examination setting as real as possible.

The mock examinations were completed in early October. Alas, however, the results were a bit disappointing! Students needed remedial training in all subjects, especially shorthand. It was all too obvious that the shorthand teacher had really not been putting forth as much effort as she tried to make me think. It was also obvious that this Forkner method was a real disaster!

I finally decided to take it upon myself to give the students extra dictation and practice during their study periods. The shorthand teacher was not too happy with this decision, and clearly showed her dissatisfaction. Since she did not extend herself to put forth any extra effort, I ignored her attitude and proceeded with my reinforcement exercises. The more I worked with the students, the more I realized what a poor choice the introduction of Forkner shorthand had been for the school. But we continued to struggle on.

Shortly after our mock examination fiasco, I was happy to welcome another visitor from the United States, my friend, Marshall Schachtman. Marshall had been a co-worker of mine, an engineer from Bell Laboratories. He had come to Kenya on a safari, and made it a point as part of his itinerary to visit our secretarial school. He couldn't have come at a better time, since I was feeling a bit "down" because of the mock examination results.

Marshall took group pictures of the secretarial students, and they really enjoyed his visit. He then topped it off by treating me to a dinner at the famous Norfolk Hotel! What a wonderful friend I had in Marshall, and still have to this day!

In early November, I began recruiting for new students at some of the other National Youth Service sites. We wanted to have a continuous influx of students to be available when the first group of students advanced to their second year so that we could continue on with a new group. I visited these sites with some of the officers from the National Youth Service. It was a great outing for me and gave me a chance to see the wonderful and beautiful countryside of Kenya! This was something I had been unable to do since coming to Kenya because of my arduous and busy schedule at the school. I made a note to myself that, someday, when my volunteer days were over, I would return to Kenya for a safari of my own.

On the way back to Nairobi, we stopped and bought fresh fruit and vegetables from roadside vendors. We also stopped to eat roasted meat as only the Kenyans can roast it. The following day, we left Nairobi again and recruited at another site. This trip was more strenuous than the first one, the roads being more bumpy and rather treacherous. Both days were rewarding, however, in that we did manage to get candidates for our school.

On November 25, 1975, the "real" East African examinations began! History was being made today! The National Youth Service secretarial students were sitting for their first Stage I, E.A.E.C. examinations! The subjects were English, commerce, and shorthand. The office practice and typewriting examinations were scheduled for the following year.

English was the first examination to be given. The teachers were tense, the students scared and jittery. Two invigilators arrived early, stoic and solemn. As was the custom, Madam Jane, the English teacher, had to leave the classroom and turn the testing over to the invigilators. The students were on their own now!

The agonizing two and one-half hours went by slowly, as Madam Jane and I sweated through the English examination. We had been given a copy of the examination after the students received theirs. Needless to say, we were quite nervous when we saw the questions that they had to answer.

Upon completion of the examination, the invigilators collected all papers, packed them in their briefcases, and left quietly. The next procedure was for the papers to be turned over the official examination council, corrected, and then a few months later we would be notified of the results.

The students poured out of the classroom, some apprehensive, some positive about their efforts. It had truly been an exciting day for them! Our next challenge, the fearful commerce examination, was scheduled for the next day.

Mr. Mburu, Madam Jane, and I arrived at school early the next morning. The students had arrived even earlier and had gone to their classrooms. The invigilators soon arrived and proceeded to pass out the commerce examination papers. They then brought copies to the teachers as we waited in the staff room.

We looked carefully at the examination papers, and then exclaimed in unison, "What is this? What is this? This is the wrong exam!" The principal read further on, then commented,

"Commercial Law? Good heavens! Ours students will panic! They don't have this course of study! What's going on?"

The invigilators quickly realized their mistake when the students began to exclaim in the classroom. The invigilators collected the examination papers and explained that they would have to go back to town and get the correct exams. They promised to return shortly.

We waited around for quite some time. We finally sent the students back to camp, since it was nearing their lunch hour. The invigilators did not return until late, very late, that evening. The commerce exam did not start until 5:45 pm! It lasted until 8:30 pm that night! Naturally, our students were exhausted. The examination had been difficult, and, coupled with the faux pas of the day, they were not too positive about their efforts. Nevertheless, we encouraged them to hope for good results.

After we dismissed the students, Mr. Mburu left for home. Madam Jane and I were given an escort home by an NYS officer. Well, another exciting and eventful day at the National Youth Service secretarial school!

On Monday, eleven students sat for their first Forkner shorthand examination. The number of candidates was low due to the slow progress the students had been making in this subject. I had previously tried to dissuade them from sitting for exams until spring, but some of them were so eager to try.

This examination consisted of 60-70 words per minute dictation, then transcribing by hand to notebooks. This was the E.A.E.C. procedure. However, when the students sat for shorthand the following year, they had been trained to transcribe their notes by using the typewriter. This first shorthand examination was, as expected, very difficult for the students.

I did all I could to calm their fears about failing and encouraged them to continue to think positive about their studies, emphasizing the fact that we would have to try harder in the future.

2ND STUDENT ENROLLMENT NYSSS 1975

Rest And Recuperation

11

When school closed for the holidays, I was given an opportunity by Peace Corps to take a two-week trip to Mombasa. The purpose of this trip was for remedial training in Kiswahili. At the end of our classes every day, we were then allowed to be on our own for rest and recuperation.

The trip to Mombasa was a 14-hour train ride. I traveled alone, however, the train was crowded with 1st, 2nd, and 3rd class passengers. The Peace Corps volunteers were given 2nd class privileges. As I eased my way through the packed train, I could see 3rd class passengers sitting on the floor, in the aisle, and in the doorways. Hundreds of them with many watoto and many live chickens. In fact, I shared my 2nd class accommodations with a mother, two children, and two live chickens!

I finally arrived in Mombasa and checked in with Peace Corps staff members. I was then sent to a moderate beach hotel with rather comfortable accommodations. Except for a few mice scurrying around and a few mice droppings now and then, I was quite satisfied. While in Mombasa, I also met a few more Peace Corps volunteers who were serving at other sites.

Kiswahili classes were five hours in length each day, and the remainder of the day we had to ourselves. The weather was extremely hot, but

Mombasa was so beautiful that the heat did not matter to me. The instructors were excellent, and finally, some of the Kiswahili did begin to come back and sink in.

The two weeks went by quickly, and my rest and recuperation trip was over. On December 19th, I took the 14-hour train ride back to Nairobi. This time my roommates consisted of another mother with her four watoto, and a few more live chickens. The watoto were well behaved, and the chickens relatively quiet.

When I returned to Westlands, I spent the remaing time leisurely. The Perry family welcomed me as usual. I spent Christmas day at their home where they lavishly entertained me and about 20 other guests.

On January 1, 1976, New Year's Day, I was picked up at home by one of my students, Margaret Kimana, and her father, David Kimana. Mr. Kimana had often visited his daughter at the secretarial school, and during the course of time, we became great friends. They took me to their home in the town of Kiambu. There I met Mrs. Kimana and the other children in the family. At their home, I feasted on delicious roasted meat, irio, fresh vegetables and fruit.

On my return trip back home, the Kimanas showed me the breathtaking surrounding savannas of Kenya. We visited markets, large farmlands, coffee, tea, and pineapple plantations where I met many friendly villagers. What a pleasant way to start the New Year! I really felt at home in Africa.

MARGARET KIMANA (FAR RIGHT) WITH HER FAMILY

Blessings

12

On January 6, 1976, school reopened, and our classes continued at a normal pace. And then in early February, we received good news! The typewriters donated by Bell Laboratories had arrived. What a blessing! They couldn't have come at a better time since Stage I typing exams were scheduled for March.

I thought that when the typewriters arrived they would be brought to the school, checked out and installed, and we would be on our way to routine class work. Not so. Receiving these typewriters from Bell Laboratories turned out to be a "big thing!" The official at NYS headquarters notified me that there was to be a special presentation of the typewriters to the school. This meant that the Permanent Secretary of the Kenya government would be coming and an official ceremony would be held. I, as principal, and also representing Bell Laboratories, would officially turn the typewriters over to the government of Kenya.

So now everyone was bustling around preparing for the big day. We spruced up the school by painting and doing extensive cleaning. There was even going to be a parade, and the students had to participate in an official march. Then there would be a reception; the whole bit!

The day of the presentation arrived. Officials were all over the place! The people of Kenya really know how to express their gratitude! A new

Peace Corps Director, William Robertson, had recently arrived when the previous director's assignment had ended. Of course, Mr. Robertson was invited to the ceremony.

The ceremony went off without a hitch. After the school staff greeted Mr. Otieno, the Minister of Labor, we witnessed a parade by the students, and then a formal inspection of the students by Mr. Otieno. The principal then turned the typewriters over to the Kenya government officials, and the program was complete. It was indeed a joyful day for the students and the entire staff!

The electric current in Kenya is different from that in the United States, 115V as compared to 220V. Therefore, adjustments had to be made in our electrical system with the installation of transformers and use of converters for the electric typewriters. Thanks to the excellent help and expertise of Rich Palas, another conscientious Peace Corps volunteer, this task was accomplished.

We were finally on our way. With ten manual typewriters received from headquarters, and about ten manuals salvaged from the Peace Cops pile, coupled with the twelve beautiful machines donated by Bell Laboratories, we were now ready to tackle the East African typewriting exams!

On March 22, 1976, the students sat for their first typewriting exams, Stage I. Talk about nail-biting! Are the machines O.K.? Hope we don't have a power failure problem with the IBM electrics. Hope the ribbons don't break. Just hope all goes well.

The invigilator brought me a copy of the typewriting exam. I shuddered. "C'est tres difficile!" A two-hour examination consisting of the following:

Exercise 1—Ten-minute timing
Exercise 2—Letter to be edited and typed
Exercise 3—Manuscript to be edited and typed
Exercise 4—Application form to be suitably displayed
Exercise 5—Table to be edited and typed with correct rulings.

Wow! What a challenge our students faced. Finally, the exams were over and the students filed out of the classroom. Some students looked completely bewildered; others seemed a bit more confident. The principal said, "All right ladies, I know you're glad this is over. Now let's put this behind us and get ready for Office Practice I, which will take place a few days from now."

The office practice examination also proved to be difficult, but Madam Beverly hung in there with words of encouragement to all the students. We had finally completed our first circle of all Stage I examinations in spite of numerous setbacks, disappointments, and other intervening variables. When I look back, I wonder how we made it. I'm sure now it was due to God's help, faith, prayer, determination, perseverance, and dedicated teachers.

Finally, with the hectic days of examinations over, we settled down to peace and quiet.. After a relaxing week-end, I reported to school early one Monday morning and, as usual, checked all the classrooms.

What's this? What's this? Something is wrong in the typing classroom. Something is missing. Typewriters, ten of them, the manual machines have disappeared!

I quickly contacted headquarters. General China and his entourage arrived at the school. General China was furious! Everyone was excited, and the students were visibly upset. The government officials took over, inspecting and checking. Utter chaos and confusion reigned for a while.

As it turned out, the thief (or thieves) was never caught. It was unbelievable! Just when everything was going along so smoothly. Thank goodness this did not happen before the typing exams took place!

Shortly after this incident, we received the official results from our first E.A.E.C. examinations. Alas! Only five passes in English, ten in commerce, three in shorthand. Needless to say the staff was disappointed, and, of course, the students were crestfallen. At least now we knew that our students could accomplish these exams in spite of their weak educational backgrounds. This, in itself, meant a lot, and our pep talks to the students intensified their desire to try harder.

But then, we received a shot in the arm! Typewriting, Stage I, and Office Practice, Stage I results came in. There were 17 passes in typewriting! There were 39 passes (out of 41) in office practice! Even with all our ups and downs, these were excellent results. As one can well imagine, the students were ecstatic! I must say, that Madam Beverly really knew her stuff with the office practice course. She deserved to be commended for all her hard work and patience. We were on our way again. Mzuri sana!

GREETING MR. OTIENO, MINISTER OF LABOR

MINISTER OF LABOR INSPECTS STUDENTS

*PRINCIPAL PRESENTS TYPEWRITERS
TO KENYA GOVERNMENT OFFICIALS*

STUDENTS ADMIRING TYPEWRITERS

Moving Right Along

13

June 1, 1976—Another Madaraka Day had rolled around! But this time the planes flew higher with no tragedies. Our students marched smartly, as usual. This time it was a beautiful Madaraka Day!

June 7,1976—Another eventful day. What joy and happiness! The National Youth Service presented the secretarial school with ten, brand new manual Olivetti typewriters! This gift was from headquarters. The men were finally beginning to turn around. They saw the light when our examination results came through, and to show their understanding and appreciation, we had been rewarded. Who said the Kenya men were cold, pessimistic, and uncaring? Not me! Not me!

All is quiet and settled again. We took the students on several commerce field trips to various industrial plants and corporations. Mr. Mburu was doing an excellent job of gathering material together and planning trips to make the commerce course more interesting.

In late June, Madam Jane took a well deserved home leave back to the United States for 30 days. As agreed, I took over her English classes until she returned. Needless to say, I learned a lot. I struggled with the teaching, however, I was never so glad to see Madam Jane when she returned from her vacation.

In July, once again it was time for E.A.E.C. examinations. This time some of the students took Stage I, while others sat for Stage II. Stage I was a repeat for those who had failed the first time. Stage II, of course, covered those students who had passed various subjects in Stage I. All of the subjects were included, English, commerce, typing, office practice, and shorthand. This time our students appeared poised and confident.

All of the exams went smoothly and were uneventful, except for shorthand. The following scenario took place on the day of the shorthand examination:

When I came to school on the day of the shorthand exam, the invigilators had not yet arrived. This was not uncommon because they were often late. By 9:30 am when the invigilators still had not arrived, I began to worry. I tried to reach Mr. Otieno, the examinations officer, by telephone. No answer. I then rang Mr. Githaiga and asked for transport to Mitihani House (examination office where Mr. Otieno was located). Mr.Githaiga informed me that transport was not available. His driver, Njiru, had just left for town and General China had left for town also.

I decided to walk up to headquarters anyway. Maybe a vehicle will be coming along. As I left the school, an NYS bus was coming from headquarters. Purity Nyambura, one of the students, runs on ahead to wave the bus down. It passes the school and does not stop. Now here comes a carryall vehicle. The driver stops, and meanwhile, the bus has finally stopped up ahead. Now, here comes the DDO, General China, in his private vehicle. His driver stops and General China offers me a lift to town.

When I arrive at Mitihani, General China says he will send a driver back for me when I am ready to leave. I hurried up to Mr. Otieno's office and met his secretary. She informs me that Mr. Otieno is not in, she doesn't know where he went, but that he will be back. I then ask her how to get in touch with the supervisor of the invigilators. Secretary rummages through her desk drawer containing piles of papers and other items, all completely in disorder. She can't find the telephone number.

By now it's 10:30 am. In walks Mr. Otieno. He greets me:

"Good morning, principal. What can I do for you?"

I then ask him, "Where are the invigilators? Our shorthand exams were scheduled for today. Two sittings, one this morning; one this afternoon."

Mr. Otieno then says, "Greet me, first, principal. Relax. Invigilators? There is no typing exam today."

I reply to him, "No, but the shorthand exam has to be transcribed by typewriters now."

Mr. Otieno then says, "Oh, yes, Mrs. Etau (the supervisor) was here on Friday. She took the exam papers with her. She said she would contact you on Saturday.

I said to him, "We're not open on Saturdays."

Mr. Otieno seems surprised. "Oh, you're not? Well, I will ring her at home. She and her sons were coming to your school as invigilators. Let's see if we can locate those chaps."

Mr. Otieno rings Mrs. Etau's home. She is not in. He then rings Mr. Etau at his office. He reaches Mr. Etau and explains the situation. Mr. Etau says he will notify his wife and sons. He will tell them to be at the school by 12 noon.

I ring Mr. Githaiga again and ask for transport. He says he will send a land rover for me. I then ring the school and leave a message that the students scheduled for the afternoon exam should return to camp. Those previously scheduled for the morning exam are to wait for the invigilators.

Mr. Otieno then says, "Everything all right? Don't worry, principal. Relax. You haven't seen anything in Kenya yet. Excuse me, I am going upstairs for tea."

I then left and went downstairs to wait for the land rover. I guess there was a change of plans, because now General China had arrived with his driver. Whatever the case, I was glad, and hopped in the vehicle for the return trip to school. When I returned to the school, the invigilators had just arrived. It was now past 12 noon.

There followed a lengthy discussion concerning the procedures to be followed. The invigilators wanted the students to take dictation, write it out, then transcribe their longhand notes to the typewriter. All in 40 minutes! I explained to them that now the students transcribe directly to the typewriter. The invigilators seemed confused, but went along with my explanation. The exam finally began at 1:00 pm.

The second group of students arrived for the afternoon session shortly after the first group began their exam. Since we were so far behind in our schedule, I sent the second group to one of the other classrooms to wait. They were also able to practice while waiting. The invigilators consented to give the students more than 40 minutes to transcribe their notes, consequently, the first exam did not end until 3:00 pm.

The afternoon group began their exam at 3:30 pm. This one didn't end until 5:30 pm., but it was finally over! I breathed a sigh of relief, and called headquarters for a vehicle to transport me and the other teachers home. What an eventful day this had been!

Home Leave

14

By now we were well into almost two years of studies at the secretarial school. Upon completion of our July exams, the students had become regular pros. After the examinations, school closed for one month. During the month of August, a full concentration is devoted to sports at the National Youth Service. Servicemen and servicewomen, including our students, participated vigorously in track, soccer, Judo, and volleyball. Competition is high and sports events can even be likened to a mini Olympics. I attended some of the sports events and thoroughly enjoyed every moment. Our National Youth Service students excelled in their sports achievements comparable to any professional athletes.

By this time, I would have been near completion of my two-year assignment in Kenya and ready to depart sometime in October, 1976. However, because of the intense challenges during these 15 months, I had submitted a request to Bell Laboratories in early March, for an extended Leave of Absence for one more year. I felt that my work here in Kenya was not quite finished. Also, I wanted to implement a smooth transition from a Peace Corps volunteer staff to a Kenyan principal and an all-Kenyan teaching staff.

Bell Laboratories granted me the one-year extension. With my one-year extension, the Peace Corps informed me that I was entitled to home leave for approximately 30 days. When Madam Jane returned from her leave on August 7th, I began making preparations for my leave. On August 9, 1976, I departed for the United States.

My trip home was pleasant. I was somewhat excited, and, at first, looked forward to the comfortable living, good food, and modern conveniences that life offered in the United States. However, within two weeks I was homesick for Kenya. My family and friends welcomed me with open arms. They went out of their way to show me a great time during my stay. Most of them, however, after the first week, clearly indicated that they were not really interested in my African experiences. Once the novelty of my returning home wore off, I found that when I started relating some events, their attention span was not really there. They still could not understand why I would want to return to Africa and continue with my rugged and arduous lifestyle. .

With the exception of a few interested friends, I soon refrained from discussing Kenya to any great length. I realized that most of my friends and relatives had no concept of Africa nor my great interest in Africa. Nor did many of them even have any idea what I was talking about when I made attempts to educate them about Africa. It was wonderful to be wined and dined extensively, and to greet old friends and neighbors, but I was still not ready to return to the so-called "real world." I could hardly wait to get on that plane and get back to my other home, Kenya!.

On September 21, 1976, I departed for Kenya to return to my school and my students.

I was anxious to get "home" and had forgotten about those seven stops; had also forgotten about those long 23 hours, but we arrived safely.

When I reached the airport I was met by four of my students and Njiru, the NYS driver. During my absence, another Peace Corps volunteer had stayed at my apartment to take care of Ripper, my cat. When I arrived home, Ripper meowed happily, and I'm sure that she, too, was glad that I had returned.

I returned to the secretarial school on September 25th. I was greeted with many warm and vigorous handshakes by my students. They were happy to see me, and I, in turn, was more than happy to see them again!

I soon settled down to my regular routine, and also concerns for the secretarial school. Within a few weeks, I contacted the Peace Corps office to discuss special secretarial and business training for some of our students. Certain students were doing so well in their studies that I conceived the idea of placing them in a working environment before they completed their two years of secretarial training at the school. I met with Mr. Robertson, the Peace Corps Director, Mark Anderson, the Associate Peace Corps Director, and Joseph Kuria, the Associate Peace Corps Director in charge of education. I had also previously contacted Mr. Griffin, our National Youth Service Director, and received his approval of my plan.

Training began at the Peace Corps office in October 1976. Two students were assigned to the Peace Corps administrative office, three days a week, Monday, Tuesday, and Wednesday. They returned to the secretarial school for regular classes on Thursday and Friday.

Two of the top scholastic students, Taffy M'Bone and Mildred Nekesa, were chosen for this secretarial training. The training consisted of receiving and placing telephone calls, typing, filing, and other related secretarial assignments as required. They were supervised and guided by Kenyan administrative personnel who were employed by the Peace Corps.

Transportation was provided daily by the National Youth Service staff bus. Lunch fees of ten shillings per day were provided by Peace Corps. This training took place for a period of one month, October through November. It was purely experimental, but proved to be very successful. These students were given a brief, but worthwhile exposure to life in the business sector, and they were able to relate their experience to the other secretarial students.

Upon completion of this one-month training, the students returned to the secretarial school, full time, in preparation for their final examinations before graduation. These students made their classmates aware of the many opportunities that awaited them upon completion of their schooling.

We were now near completion of the two-year secretarial training at the school. The entire teaching staff began to get ready for the final examinations in Stages I and II. We had become adjusted to setbacks, surprises, and just about any event that could occur during these hectic times. The final examination period was from November 16 through November 25, 1976. For the first time, everything went smoothly. There were no hitches, no machine breakdowns, no mix-up in dates or examination papers. When exams were over, we spent a few days getting our second wind, and then began preparations for our first graduation.

Graduation

15

The great day had finally arrived! December 7, 1976! We were honored with the presence of the Honorable S. T, Kairo, Member of Parliament, as the guest of honor. Other dignitaries included our Peace Corps Director, Mr. William Robertson, the NYS Director, Mr. G. W. Griffin, Mr. Gower, and other staff officers of the National Youth Service. There was a grand salute by the NYS servicewomen, and inspection of the honor guard.

Mr. Kairo presented the graduation certificates, followed by his personal address, which was warming and inspiring. Servicewoman Mildred Nekesa, one of the top students, delivered an address of thanks on behalf of the graduating class. I, as principal, then presented the following report on the history and progress of the secretarial school:

"Most significantly, is the outstanding achievement that these young women have made. This is a momentous and great occasion for them. It is also a happy and self-rewarding period for the entire teaching staff. The dedication and hard work on their part can never be over-emphasized. We, as teachers, can look back on some of the events that took place and wonder how we overcame so many obstacles. Nevertheless, we did, and now we can smile about what appeared then to be insurmountable challenges.

As for the students, well, I have never seen such a more meaningful interpretation of harambee as that exhibited by these young women over the past two years. The "pulling together" of both staff and students resulted in outstanding achievements. I would now like to share with you the results of our two years of training and successful accomplishments:

SUBJECT	No. of Students Taking Exam	No. of Passes
COMMERCE—STAGE I	44	37
COMMERCE—STAGE II	29	13
ENGLISH—STAGE I	44	28
ENGLISH—STAGE II	9	8
OFFICE PRACTICE—STAGE I	44	42
OFFICE PRACTICE—STAGE II	37	9
SHORTHAND—STAGE I	44	23
SHORTHAND—STAGE II	11	3
TYPEWRITING—STAGE I	44	35
TYPEWRITING—STAGE II	26	15

It is with a deep sense of pride and joy that I present this report. It represents two years of struggle and tremendous effort on the part of the students. I am sure that you will all join me in giving these young women a standing ovation."

A reception followed the graduation ceremonies. When all was over, both students and staff left the school that day totally elated. Truly our goals had been reached successfully!

SCHOOL SONG
(Written by Students and Presented at
Graduation Ceremonies)

Our hearts rejoice as round you we gather
To offer you our wishes best
And God help you teachers
With heavenly gifts both rare and blest.

You came to Kenya to brighten our future
Our foreheads shine with what you have taught us.
We'll try to impart it to our brothers and sisters
Your work will shine from day to day.

May sorrow and grief never afflict you,
But grateful love surround you each day
Your wisdom guide you to peace and unity
Your loving care, may God repay.

We thank our Directors and Mr. Gower
For their idea of forming the school.
We now have acquired what we deserve
So now we pray for them a long life.

The Peace Corps is also remembered
For what it has done for NYS
We all welcome you, and also our guests
To enjoy this great day with us.

GRADUATION DAY–DECEMBER 7, 1976

Memorable Occasions

16

After graduation, school closed and most of the students prepared for holiday leave. The shorthand teacher, having completed her two-year assignment, returned to the United States in mid-December. Plans for replacement were already in effect, and we expected a new Peace Corps volunteer the early part of the year.

I, along with the remaining staff members, welcomed a respite from the school year, and we too, made preparations for our holidays. My husband, Theodore (Ted) Holimon, a captain with the Asbury Park Police Department, retired from his position while I was living and working in Kenya. After much persuasion, I convinced him that he should make a trip to Kenya. Just prior to the Christmas holidays, he came over. During his visit, I finally managed to enjoy a Kenya safari, my first. Another friend of mine, Martha Whiting, who worked in Kenya under the CARE program, made arrangements for Ted and me to take a safari trip to Mount Kenya. Martha and I had become very good friends during my stay in Kenya.

We visited Mt. Kenya, and spent two pleasant days at the Ark Lodge. We also made a trip to Nakuru to view the Great Rift Valley and the spectacular pink flamingoes, two popular tourist attractions.

During Ted's brief visit, I invited a few of the National Youth Service staff members an some of my other Kenyan friends to my home. Ted and I planned the food for this occasion. Ted had always done most of the cooking back in the States, so he was happy to prepare the meal for this occasion. While we were preparing for the festivities, one of the Kenyans, Mr. Kimana, arrived early. He was surprised, and I might even say, horrified, to find Ted in the kitchen preparing the food. "What is he doing in the kitchen, he asked. Our men never enter the kitchen. They are not supposed to help with the cooking."

During the festivities, when the American men and women served themselves, the Kenyan men were astounded. According to their custom, women must always serve the men first before even thinking about serving themselves. Well, the men of Kenya learned a lot that day. We joked about it considerably, but when they departed, they were still shaking their heads in disbelief and disapproval, each mumbling to himself in his own particular tribal language.

While visiting my home, each ethnic group had spoken their own language, interspersed with English. Ted could not get over this. He commented that, although the Africans were similar to us in appearance, most of the time he could not understand a word they were saying. But he enjoyed his stay and left Kenya with a warm feeling towards the people of Africa. He, too, felt happy that he had visited the motherland at least once in his lifetime.

Another memorable occasion occurred a few months after Ted left Kenya. On February 26, 1976, the officers and staff of the National Youth Service were invited by President Jomo Kenyatta to attend a special ceremony in Nakuru. The purpose of our visit was to receive special commendations from the president on the fine work and performance that had been exhibited by the National Youth Service.

President Kenyatta gave a welcoming speech and thanked us for the wonderful progress the National Youth Service had made. He then presented us with a special certificate for our efforts and dedication. Of course, we were all very excited and grateful for this special audience. I never thought that some day in my life I would be shaking hands with His Excellency, President Jomo Kenyatta! This visit will always be etched in my memories of Kenya as one of my cherished moments.

Shortly after the trip to Nakuru, I once again welcomed visitors from the United States. This time, another Bell Laboratories co-worker, David Carson and his wife, Marilyn, along with some other travelers, were on safari in Kenya. In what was getting to be a trend from all my visitors, they treated me to dinner at the Hilton Hotel where they were staying. We spent a pleasant evening together before they continued on their holiday journey. How fortunate I was to have such great Bell Laboratories' friends!

And then another memorable occasion! As previously mentioned, my cat, Ripper finally had a small litter in May of 1977, four beautiful kittens. I kept two of the kittens and gave the other two away. When I returned to the states I brought Ripper and the two kittens back with me. During that long flight back to the states, I alighted from the plane at each of the seven stops, sat under the wing of the plane while it was loading and unloading to make sure that my "family" was safe.

The next occasion that is still etched in my mind is attendance at a Kikuyu wedding. Shortly before Madam Jane completed her assignment at the secretarial school, she and I were invited to attend this wedding by one of my substitute teachers, Mr. Waruingi, who was getting married.

The wedding took place on a Saturday afternoon at a large church. There were hundreds of guests, and we were warmly welcomed by them. The wedding ceremony, although in the Kikuyu language, had all the resemblance of our regular Christian ceremony, so we had no difficulty following the service. After the ceremony, we left for the reception which was held nearby in a large picnic-type area. Of course, there was lots of food, especially irio, the basic dish of the Kikuyu people, roasted meat, fresh vegetables, and all kinds of sweets.

A Kikuyu reception, like many other African wedding receptions, calls for a long dissertation by one of the elders, usually the father of the bride. The elder stands before the bridal party and guests, and, while giving his speech, special gifts, in addition to the regular wedding gifts, are displayed. The special gifts consist of a spade, a rake, a hoe, a shovel, a water carrier, and various other tools associated with tending a farm. These gifts are presented to the bride, and she is told that she will be expected to use them accordingly.

The final special gift is then presented, a bed. A bed is actually brought out, set up and covered with the proper bed linen. The bride is then told that she will be expected to use this bed by providing many children, especially boys, to the groom. Although this part of the cere-mony produces much laughter and comments, the intent is serious and not taken lightly.

Although the elder spoke in Kikuyu, the message came over very clearly. Indeed, this was an interesting and enlightening exposure to a Kikuyu wedding.

TED ENJOYING AFRICAN SUNSHINE

TIROKO (MASSAI FRIEND) AND TED

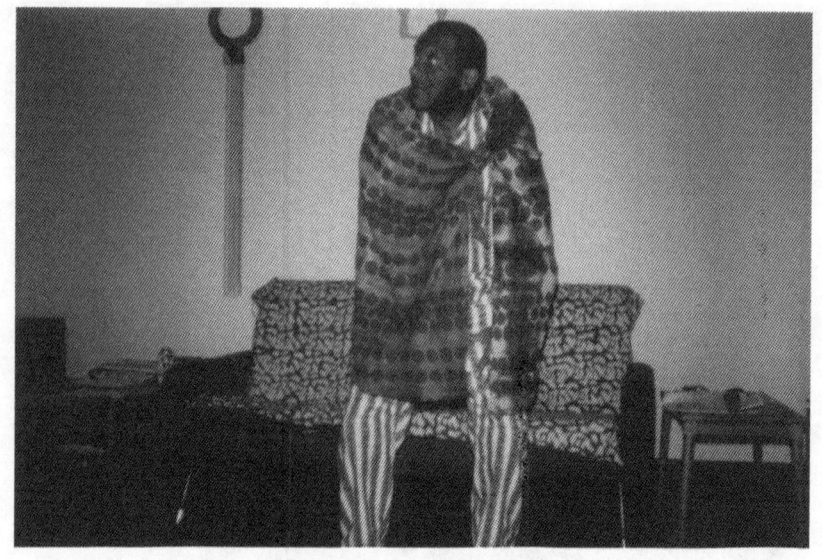

MAKING LIKE A MAASAI

TED AND RAINETTE AT THE ARK
MT. KENYA

HIS EXCELLENCY, PRESIDENT JOMO KENYATTA

AN AUDIENCE WITH HIS EXCELLENCY,
PRESIDENT JOMO KENYATTA

Departure Time

17

When the students returned from holiday in early 1977, the graduates were confronted with a busy schedule. They were still members of the National Youth Service, and although no longer attending the secretarial school, were still housed at the compound. Now they were concentrating on finding jobs with the government or within the private sector. This entailed tremendous preparation for numerous job interviews.

The first enrollment of secretarial students all graduated upon completion of their two years of training. If, after two years, they had still failed in some subjects, they continued their studies on their own. Then they applied directly to the East African Examinations Council to repeat any of the exams they had failed.

Before I left the National Youth Service secretarial school in December 1977, all of the students from our pioneer graduating class had been placed in positions with the government or private sector.

We were now settling down to our regular schedule. There were, however, a few changes in the teaching staff. Mrs. Robertson, a white American Peace Corps volunteer, had just completed four years of service in Ghana. She joined us and became the Pitman shorthand teacher. Yes, Peace Corps had finally realized that the Forkner system was not working satisfactorily. The students welcomed the challenge and eagerly looked forward to learning the Pitman method.

In August, 1977, Madam Beverly completed her Peace Corps service at the secretarial school. We were sorry to see her leave. She had done such a wonderful job with the students in both typewriting and office practice. Her examination results had been exemplary throughout her entire two years.

When Madam Beverly left, she was replaced by a Kenyan, Mrs. L. Plapan. Mrs. Plapan was a fully qualified commercial teacher, and we were happy to have her on board. Now I could, once again, concentrate on my role as principal.

It had been previously determined by Peace Corps that, eventually, replacements for all Peace Corps volunteers at the secretarial school would be filled by Kenyans. Consequently, Peace Corps felt that our role as volunteers had been fulfilled, and that the Kenyans were now capable of assuming full responsibility for the school. I had been grooming Mr. Mburu, the commerce teacher, for the role of principal. Of course, he would have to go through the procedure of applying and interviewing, but I strongly supported him as the choice to replace me.

However, another catastrophe soon occurred at the school. Mrs. Plapan, the typing teacher, after only one month with us, asked for a transfer to another government school. This came as quite a blow, since our curriculum had been rearranged to give her full responsibility over the typing classes. I had continued with the office practice course so that Mrs. Plapan could devote all of her time to typewriting instructions.

So then, what transpired now? Why the principal, along with her other duties, went back to teaching typing again! When Mrs. Plapan notified me of her transfer plans, I quickly submitted a request to the Permanent Secretary for a replacement. This position, however, was not filled before my final departure from the secretarial school.

All good things must come to an end, and finally, Madam Jane, my "right hand" completed her Peace Corps assignment in September 1977. I cannot begin to express my feelings towards Madam Jane in her role as teacher, counselor, advisor, and pioneer volunteer of the secretarial school. You name it; she was all of these. Again, I stress the fact that without her dedication and support, my role as principal of the school would not have been a successful one.

Although Madam Jane's departure was inevitable and had been anticipated, it was with deep sorrow that I and the students bade her farewell. When she left, Mr. Mburu then took over the English classes. Mr. Ngugi, another Kenyan, came to the school to teach commerce.

As the time drew near for my departure, I gave Mr. Mburu more and more responsibilities in assuming the role of principal. He had not been officially appointed as principal of the school to replace me, since there was much government "red tape" in filling this position. A number of candidates had to be considered and interviewed. The final decision would be made by officials from the Ministry of Labor. Nevertheless, before leaving in December, 1977, I officially turned the keys over to Simon Peter Mburu, thus making him Acting Principal of the National Youth Service Secretarial School.

My departure was quiet, without a lot of fanfare, as I so requested. In early December, I met with the director, Mr. Griffin, and other officials from National Youth Service headquarters, for a brief conference and to report the status of the school. All was in order, and the transition of Mr. Mburu as acting principal was completed.

Then came a tearful farewell to my students. I was still not ready to leave Kenya, even after three and one-half years, but I knew I had to return to my company in the United States. My task was over. It had been a wonderful and rewarding experience. I know that with God's help I was able to accomplish what seemed sometimes to be insurmountable odds. Truly, in retrospect, I can say that these were the "best years of my life." Kenya yetu, my "home" away from home.

When I returned to the states, I continued to correspond with Mr. Mburu and some of my former students. In 1978, Mr. Mburu, now as principal, presented the second graduation class for the National Youth Service secretarial school. He sent me a full report with very commendable examination results.

In the fall of 1980, one of my former students, Florence Nekesa, who was now married, informed me that she had given birth to a baby girl. Her choice of a name for her firstborn was "Rainette." I was overwhelmed! It breaks tradition for an African to choose a name for their child, especially the firstborn, that is not an African name. I felt honored.

BEVERLY, SIMON, JANE

Kenya Revisited

18

Kenya, 1983—Excerpts taken from an article by my hometown newspaper, the Asbury Park Press, read as follows:

City Woman Sees Price of Progress

The school she helped found in the Republic of Kenya is now a vacant lot, but Rainette B. Holimon understands that progress comes with a price. About a mile from the former National Youth Service Secretarial School is the new National Youth Service Secretarial College and Upholstery School. It has double the number of classrooms and can accommodate four times the number of students.

On Decembr 6, 1983, His Excellency, the Honorable Daniel T. Arap Moi, new president of Kenya, presided at the opening of the National Youth Service Secretarial College, Ruaraka, Kenya. Mrs. Holimon had received a special invitation from the president to attend the opening ceremonies.

"What a thrilling experience," Mrs. Holimon said about the trip. "I was met at Jomo Kenyatta International Airport by two Kenyan government officials, and driven to the National Youth Service school grounds. What had started out as a trial venture to train the young, deprived women of Kenya towards more meaningful and gainful employment, had now burgeoned and developed into a prestigious secretarial college with a waiting list of eager applicants," she said. "The National Youth Service secretarial college is playing a significant role in improving the standards of living for many future Kenyan families. I like to think that I also played a significant role in this venture. The college is more sophisticated, more modern, and has a much larger staff, so it makes it easier insofar as teaching is concerned. Nevertheless, I still have sentiment for the old school. I felt very sad when I saw the empty lot , since the building, which was once the original secretarial school, had been torn down."

From 1974 to 1983, 323 students were graduated from the secretarial school, and 323 found employment. Instead of four teachers and the principal (originally all Peace Corps volunteers) there is a principal, deputy principal, 13 academic staff members and six support staff members. Two of the staff members are graduates from the original school. There are eight classrooms, six staff offices, three main offices, a library, a language laboratory, a staff room, a typewriter workshop, and a duplicating room. Students attend the college all year for two years. The only interruption is three weeks in December.

The Peace Corps assignment is over, but the commitment remains for Mrs. Holimon. "I got my fulfillment out of it, she said. I still like to teach and spend a lot of time encouraging young people to stay in school and get a good education."

(This article by Bob Ware, Press Staff Writer)

In November 1988, I took a full vacation back to Africa. Dr. Cynthia Perry, the Peace Corps consultant during my assignment in Kenya, has been appointed Ambassador to Sierra Leone, and she had invited me to visit her. Little did I know at this time that I would return to Sierra Leone a few years later on another Peace Corps assignment.

While preparing my itinerary, I decided to include Kenya in my travels. I was anxious to see my friends and visit the school once more. Thus, I made a complete circuit in my travels. First, a visit to West Germany to see my nephew, John R. Dickerson, Jr., then a ten-day trip to Kenya; next a two-day stopover in Abidjan, then a ten-day visit with the Ambassador in Sierra Leone.

The visit to Sierra Leone was pleasant. Ambassador Perry and her family went out of their way to show me a wonderful time. My most exciting experience was the return to Kenya once again.

What changes had taken place since my last visit in 1983! The National Youth Service Secretarial College and Upholstery School had merged with the Kenya Government Secretarial College in 1988. At that time, His Excellency, President Moi, had upgraded the secretarial school to a secretarial college because of the excellent work and examination performance by the students. At the time of upgrading, the college had approximately 150 students. There were 15 teachers and 15 support staff members. The merger increased the teaching staff to 30 and the support staff to 30. The school enrollment had increased to 250!

The National Youth Service secretarial school had, indeed, come a long way since 1974.

On this trip in 1983, I visited two of my former students, Purity Nyambura, and Florence Nekesa. Purity was now married with a family of three children. Florence was teaching typing at the NYS secretarial college. Her family had now increased to two since the birth of her first born, Rainette. I also visited with Mr. Mburu and his family, and was entertained royally by them and some of my other students and Kenyan friends. It was indeed a wonderful welcome that was given to me on my return trip to Kenya.

WITH PURITY NYAMBURA

*FLORENCE NEKESA
WITH HER CHILDREN
RAINETTE AND TITUS*

PART TWO
Iran

The Ugly American

19

When I returned to the United States, I reported to Bell Laboratories for a new assignment. From January to mid-April, assumed the position of Consultant for various secretarial training workshops. It was just a fill-in until I was able to find something more stable within the company.

While I had been away in Kenya, my parent company, American Telephone and Telegraph, had undertaken a communications contract with the country of Iran. AT&T had formed a new company called American Bell, International, and they were looking for candidates to fill certain positions in Iran.

So what did I do? Being a world traveler by now, I applied for a position with American Bell. I was ready to leave the country again! After an extensive interview in the states, I was finally accepted for a position in Tehran, Iran. In April 1978, I departed for Iran with the title of Personnel Recruiter and Coordinator.

The idea of going to another foreign country was, indeed, exciting. Although not Africa, the thrill of a new international experience was great. When I was accepted for this position, it took me less than ten days to prepare for the new venture. I was soon on my way!

When I arrived in Tehran, Iran, I was pleased with the luxurious and comfortable housing that was offered. All of the American Bell employees were situated in the northern part of Iran, a rather exclusive section of the country. The decision to place us in this area proved to be wise, in view of the events that were to occur later.

Driving conditions in Tehran were extremely hazardous, so we, as employees, were taxied to work each day. A contract had been set up between American Bell and the various taxi companies to transport us to and from work. Food and other supplies were plentiful, but expensive. However, it was necessary for us to boil our water and go through a sterilization process when preparing fresh fruits and vegetables. Having been accustomed to some of these precautions in Africa, it presented no problem to me, but many of the Americans had difficulty adjusting to these procedures.

Since I was living in a luxurious apartment, there were two types of toilet facilities available. They included the regular western style, with the upright commode, or the Iranian style whereby the commode was the hole-in-the-floor type similar to what I had experienced in Africa. The difference in the Iranian type, however, was that the hole was surrounded with expensive marble tile, not the dirt hole common in rural Africa. The toilet contained a bidet which could be used for cleaning one's hands and other parts of the body, and it also had the regular sink that is common in our western toilets.

We were given the privilege of furnishing our own apartments at the expense of American Bell. Social life was limited to dining out occasionally. Other social activities were confined to our individual living quarters.

The Iranians are a deeply religious group, and their custom of conduct and attire were completely different from those of the Americans. We were constantly reminded to conduct ourselves in a "laid back" manner, and also told to use discretion in our form of dress. Shorts and scant summer attire were restricted to our living quarters, and were not to be worn in the street or other public places. Most of the women of Tehran wore chadoras, a long garment which covered their entire bodies and part of their face. Iranian women who were in the working environment, however, often wore western type attire similar to that of the Americans and Europeans.

Shortly after arriving in Iran, we were enrolled in a Farsi language class. The purpose of these classes was to familiarize us Americans with the universal language of the country. Very little English was spoken by the general public, including the taxi cab drivers who transported us back and forth to work each day. All the streets and directional signs in the country were in the Farsi language.

Our classes were composed of ten people. Unfortunately, these classes were of short duration, because, with the exception of myself and two other persons, the other Americans were not interested in taking the classes. As is so often the case, the American feels that he/she does not need to learn another language. To them, English is the only way to go. In my opinion, however, the Farsi language was just too difficult for them and they did not want to take the time to learn it.

The lack of language communication proved to be a serious drawback during our stay in Iran. It also proved to be a detriment when our American Bell staff members sat down to negotiate contractual agreements, since none of the American staff could speak or understand Farsi.

There were approximately 40,000 foreigners working for various companies throughout Iran during the period that I worked there. These companies, like American Bell, International, were involved in projects geared to help improve the country. Salaries were high, and work for the foreigners was plentiful.

During my initial interview, before going to Iran, I had been told that most of the clerical positions at American Bell, International, were going to be given to the Iranians. This was to help the economy of the country, and thus give the lower income Iranians employment with American Bell.

When I arrived in Tehran, however, to my astonishment, these plans for employing the Iranians had changed. Instead of hiring the Iranians for the clerical positions, wives and older children of American Bell executives and linemen had been placed in these jobs. Anticipated employment of Iranians had been changed. Many of these wives had not worked for 30 years or more. But the promise of tax-free employment for those whose salaries were $15,000 a year, or less (a category that many of the clerical positions fell under)was too inviting for the Americans. They wanted these jobs for themselves.

So, instead of, maybe 20 or 30 clerical positions being given to the Americans, and 200 or more to the Iranians, it turned out to be just the opposite. American housewives and dependents, totaling 200 or more, were given most of the clerical positions and the remaining 20 or 30 positions were handed to the Iranians. At one point, I tried to recruit a young Iranian woman for a clerical position in my office, but was stymied in my efforts, and the job was given to a young American dependent of one of the executives.

This was a constant practice that I personally witnessed during my short stay in Iran. There were very few minority employees with American Bell in Tehran. From our company contingent of more than one thousand employees, I would venture to say that there were less than 15 black Americans, technical and/or non-technical. These were high paying jobs in Tehran, and the minorities were offered only a very small slice of the pie.

I also experienced some of that same racial resentment that I had undergone in Kenya during my confrontations with the first Peace Corps volunteer teachers. I was in a supervisory position in Iran, and some of the employees, in particular, those wives who had not worked for years, resented my authority. Although this was a different country, the white American mentality, in many instances, was still as warped as ever.

I must say here that during my many travels through Europe and Africa, nowhere, I mean nowhere, did I witness situations such as those in Iran where the Americans were so "ugly." Nowhere have I ever seen such evidence of malice and greed as that exhibited by the Americans. The term "ugly American" really fit the description while we were in Iran. No wonder we are hated in so many countries.

Troubled Times

20

As time progressed, I tried to adjust to the evidence of nepotism that strongly existed within the American Bell company. Political conditions were changing so rapidly, however, that I had little time to worry about this situation.

I had arrived in Iran in April, 1978. Within a few months after my arrival, the country was in trouble. As time passed, serious political unrest began to unfold. I was not privy to the intricacies of the various political problems that began to occur. I hesitate to express any personal opinions or comments on the events that led to our eventually leaving Iran. I was given a management position, and endeavored to follow it out during my brief assignment in Iran. I was not versed in the many chain of events, nor do I want to cast any judgment concerning them. I cannot speak on the forces that escalated the trouble in the country. I can only describe, briefly, my encounter with certain incidents that took place.

As the days passed, changes began to occur. Television shows that had been shown in English, mostly sitcom re-runs, began to go off the air. Gradually, programs were televised in Farsi only. Later on, most programs were discontinued entirely. Rumors were rampant:

There was talk that the Shah of Iran was sick, and that he was going to America. American Bell and other foreign companies were folding up and leaving the country; a person by the name of Ayatollah Khomeni was returning to Iran and would be taking over the country in place of the Shah. Countless rumors persisted and a sense of trouble and danger permeated throughout the city of Tehran.

In September, 1978, we were issued an American Bell bulletin concerning the unrest in the country. In essence, we as Americans, living in a strange country, were told to keep a low profile and not discuss any of the rumors that were floating around.

By now, martial law had been imposed in Iran, and many companies were beginning to pull out of the country. American Bell was still trying to conduct business as usual. There were constant meetings with Iranian government officials pertaining to the contract that American Bell had entered into with the country of Iran.

In early November, 1978, I made a business trip to the United States. Before returning to Iran, I contacted my supervisor at American Bell in Iran to inquire as to whether or not I should return, since by now serious trouble seemed imminent within the country. She told me that conditions were safe and that I should return to my assignment in Iran.

I returned to Iran in late November. When I arrived at the airport, I was met by two of my co-workers with whom I had become friendly with. They informed me that we had to hurry from the airport, since, by now, a 9:00 pm curfew had been imposed throughout the city. Anyone caught on the streets after 9:00 pm would be picked up by the Iranian police.

We had less than one-half hour to make it to my apartment, and then, my co-workers to their home. One can imagine what a frightful ride that was through the town, but we made it!

When I reported to work the following Monday, I could quickly see that all was not as well as had been reported to me, in fact, conditions had worsened. We were now being driven to work in curtain-drawn vans, since our popularity as Americans had begun to wane. Helicopters were flying over the city all day, searching for what I don't know, but constantly searching. Even to this day, when I hear a helicopter overhead in the United States, I am reminded of that constant droning of helicopters over the city of Tehran.

The excitement of working in a foreign country and making so much money was beginning to fade for a lot of the Americans. Many of the American Bell employees, and those with other American companies, were still reluctant to leave because of the high salaries they were getting. But gradually, fear won out over greed, and various companies began to fold.

Soon, there began a constant feeling of tenseness in our work environment. One day, as we were all working in our offices, shots rang out in the street below us. After a few moments, our director called all of us together in a small room, away from the office windows.

I must commend the director for the calm manner in which he talked to us, even as the shots were ringing out nearby. He spoke softly, but forcefully, trying to allay our fears. After about 30 minutes, the gunfire ceased. We later learned that Iranian soldiers had been pursuing two thieves, but at the time the shots rang out we didn't know if all hell had broken loose in the city of Tehran or not!

Chaos

21

We were now into early December, and the country was in complete chaos. As previously mentioned, the Iranians are very religious people, and the month of December is an extremely religious month. Many work days were canceled because a lot of Iranian prophets are commemorated during this month.

The 9:00 pm curfew was in full force by now. All lights throughout the entire city were out by 9:00 pm and all civilians had to be off the streets. Soldiers roamed the streets looking for curfew violators. Even though the curfew was in existence, every night thousands of Iranians came out and went to their particular mosque to pray. At night, many of us ventured to the rooftops of our buildings where we could stand inside the high rooftops unnoticed.

We listened, fearfully, as the Iranians began their eerie religious chanting in utter darkness. Now and then we could hear gun shots ring out as soldiers tried to disperse the crowds gathered around the mosque. This would go on every night for about an hour. Then, silence, and complete darkness, until 5:00 am the next morning.

At 7:00 am each day, our heavily curtained vans continued to arrive and take us to work. The vans became quieter each day, and there were more and more empty seats. Many of the wives of the executives and linemen were beginning to leave the country. Tempers in the office were short, and profound tenseness filled the air.

During the Christmas season things were not too merry in Iran. We had been told not to display lights or too many Christmas decorations. The low profile we had been told to keep was getting to be almost underground level.

A group of employees had been planning a trip to Bangkok for the Christmas holidays. The trip went off as planned, but by the time they were scheduled to return, the crisis in Iran had worsened. Consequently, when their vacation time was up, these employees were transported to Athens, and later returned to the United States, never to come back to Iran to resume their jobs.

January, 1979 was a chaotic month. By now, all of us American Bell employees had been told that we had to leave the country. Strong rumors indicated that the Shah of Iran had already left for his own safety, and was in the United States. The local newspapers were scream-ing with headlines every day: **"Countdown for Khomeini;" "Back to the Brink—Heavy Toll as Battle Rages near University;" "Iran Govt. Clears Way for Khomeini to Return;" "Bloody Sunday—At Least 30 Killed and Over 300 Injured; "Airports Sealed Off Till Sunday."**

Originally, the only holdup in our return to the states was the arrangement of flights for our departure. American Bell planned to keep a small skeleton force in Iran, but most of us were scheduled to return to the states as soon as possible. In late January, many flights to the states had been put into place, and most of the remaining American Bell employees were scheduled to leave Tehran.

Our company had formed a special group of employees known as the "Packing Crew." Their job was to check each employee's apart-ment and assist with packing our belongings. Iranians had also been hired to help with this project. During this time, American Bell and other companies were still on friendly terms with the Iranian government, and the government was assisting us in our departure.

Early one morning, a convoy of approximately 40 vans moved out. Our destination was the airport. We were escorted, in almost total darkness, by the Iranian military. Slowly, but stealthily, we departed. While en route to the airport, we were stopped and forced to turn back. All of a sudden the airport had been closed down! All commercial flights in and out of Tehran had been canceled!

What were we to do? Our apartments were no longer available and all of our belongings had been packed with the exception of the articles we had in our carryon luggage. Slowly, and again, stealthily, we returned to the city, but this time to the Shah Abas administrative office to await further instructions.

At Shah Abas, we were informed that all employees were to be housed at the Crown Hyatt Hotel in Tehran until further notice. We were assured that the airport would reopen in a few days, and we could then depart.

So here we were, about 1000 employees, all packed and ready to leave, with no place to go. Another 100 employees, who had been scheduled for later flights, were also sent to the Crown Hyatt. In other words, no one was allowed to return to their apartments, and all employees were placed in the hotel until further notice.

Those with pets were allowed to bring their pets to the hotel. I had a small kitten, named Ziba, and I had planned to bring her back with me to the states. Unfortunately, by the time we left Tehran after many weeks of stress and worry, so many changes had occurred. We were finally forced to leave our pets in Tehran. We were told that they would be sent to kennels for safekeeping and care. However, I learned later that most of the pets were destroyed after we left.

The American Bell staff administrators tried to make things as comfortable as possible for its employees while we were housed in the hotel. Food and liquor, previously left in employees' apartments, were brought to the hotel, and a hospitality room was set up for our convenience. We were allowed to use this room most of the day and night. We were all under quite a strain. Everyday flights were scheduled for various departures, and everyday the flights were canceled.

By now it had been confirmed that the Shah of Iran was, indeed, in the United States, safe and sound. Many employees were beginning to show signs of panic, fearful that perhaps we would not be able to get out of the country.

Within a week after the hospitality room opened, problems arose. The American Bell employees were getting out of hand, taking advantage of the free liquor and all-day use of the hospitality room.

Finally, the vice-president of our company called a special meeting for all employees. It was in the form of a breakfast to gather us all together in a pleasant atmosphere. But his speech was far from pleasant. He literally lambasted us for acting like "ugly" Americans, walking through the hotel lobby carrying cans of beer, using the hospitality room for excessive drinking, and exhibiting rude behavior toward the Iranian employees. Yes, he agreed, we were all under a strain. This was understandable, but he thought our behavior was completely obnoxious and had gotten out of control.

Consequently, the hours for use of the hospitality room were curtailed, and employees were asked to improve their behavior. I later learned that, after most of us had departed from the Crown Hyatt, the hotel was invaded by angry Iranians. One of their first acts was to destroy all the liquor that had been stored in the hospitality room.

As it turned out, we stayed at the hotel for approximately three weeks. By now, the Ayatollah Khomeini was in Tehran, the Shah was long gone, and we were still waiting to get out of Iran!

Evacuation

22

After continuous negotiations back and forth for what seemed like ages, we were finally told one day that we would soon be leaving for the airport again. Only this time there were no scheduled flights. Arrangements had been made for the United States military to take us out.

So once again, the convoys assembled early in the morning, and again, we quietly departed with an Iranian military escort leading us out of the city. Our vans were very, very quiet. We were frightened, to say the least, but everything went smoothly and orderly. When we arrived at the airport, there were thousands of people standing around They were from many different companies, all waiting to leave Iran.

We waited at the airport for hours, not really knowing when we would be leaving, and not knowing when our names would be called. As we waited, fearfully, we could see Iranian pilots practicing take-offs in F-16s on a nearby runway. And then, a sight I will long remember, a most beautiful sight! Off in the distance, the approach of a United States Air Force plane! What a sight to behold! What was even more beautiful to me, as the plane drew closer, I could see that the pilot was a black American! This was the first time I had ever seen a black American pilot in all the years I had traveled in and outside the United

States! During my travels in and out of Africa it was not uncommon to see an African pilot, but never a black American pilot. To this day, I have still yet to see a black American commercial airline pilot.

About three hours later, a number of us were permitted to board our plane, a C-141 transport. It was not the luxurious commercial airplane we had come over in, but it was a way out, and we were thankful. We were seated on the plane, backs against the wall, the way troops travel, but we were up, up and away! We had been told that our first stop would be Athens, Greece, for rest and recuperation, and then on to the United States.

When we arrived in Athens, I was given a beautiful room with a picturesque view of the Parthenon. We spent two days in Athens, shopping and sightseeing. Then a comfortable flight on TWA airlines and I was home again, back in the United States!

We who departed when we did were the lucky ones. About two weeks after our departure, the Crown Hyatt was hit hard. Some of the American Bell employees had remained to continue with packing arrangements and other logistics. One of these employees had to actually bribe armed followers of the Ayatollah Khomeini to allow him and 150 passengers to leave Iran. In return for the bribe, the soldier in charge escorted them in a lead car, accompanied by sub-machine gun protection, to Mehrabad Airport.

And, of course, later on there was the much-publicized event of Americans, under the jurisdiction of the United States Embassy, who were held hostage for a long period of time in Iran.

Although my stay in Iran was short, I did make a few new friends. In particular, two black Americans, Margaret White and her husband Cliff. We became fast friends during our short stay. Margaret and I were together on the C-141 transport when we were evacuated. Cliff, being in the military at that time, remained a little longer, but eventually, he too, returned to the states. I will always cherish their friendship.

Before the big upheaval in Iran, my friend, Marshal Schachtman, who had previously visited me in Kenya, was now an American Bell employee. He came over on a short business trip, and as usual, treated me to a delicious home-cooked Iranian meal! Good old Marshall, my friend always!

My views of Iran? The brief exposure, ten months to be exact, to the Iranian culture was warm and friendly, even up until the day of my departure. I can recall my landlord and his wife crying and asking me why I had to leave. I could only say that I was an American, and it was time for us to go. Also, in spite of the ugliness on the part of some of the Americans, not all of them were that way.

The country was beautiful, but in chaos. I only regret that events forced me to leave so abruptly, and under such sad conditions. The Iranians I met were warm and friendly. The experience was enlightening, and I have never regretted my venture. Again, it was a home away from home, if only for a short period of time.

During the early part of December, 1978, when things were beginning to boil over, I composed the following poem:

CHRISTMAS IN IRAN
(A Poem by Rainette B. Holimon)

'Twas three weeks before Christmas and all hell broke loose!
The Iranians are praying and the man wants to vamoose!
Last night was a "ringer" and that's not all I'm told
There are eight more days before the chains unfold.

The man is scared, there's no doubt about it
But he's also a trip when it comes to his pocket.
He's not going to leave until he's made his dollar
No matter how many nights the Iranians holler.
Eight months in this country and it's not too bad.
The Iranians are troubled, and also very sad.
Their palace is crumbling, the jobs are few
And what they're getting is not what they're due.

"Americans go home," they say, and it's no wonder
The way the man treats them is enough to cause thunder.
Maybe Christmas will give the Americans time to say,
"Perhaps WE should get on OUR knees and pray.]
Perhaps we'll even decide not to stay."

I wish the crying and moaning would cease
This kind of religion will never bring peace.
The experience is a challenge, but the crises are long
And Christmas in Iran doesn't promise a song.

_____Tehran, Iran (12/3/78)

RAINETTE HOLIMON & MARSHALL SCHACHTMAN IN TEHRAN, IRAN

PART THREE
Sierra Leone

Second Peace Corps Venture

23

When I came back to the United States in 1979, I returned to my company, AT&T Bell Laboratories, and once again, settled down in the corporate world. I was fortunate enough to get an Affirmative Action position in the area of university relations. This position was called the Summer Research Program, and involved heavy recruiting at various colleges in search of minority engineering students for technical employment with Bell Laboratories.

I was the coordinator of this program, and in this position, was instrumental in paving the way for many minority college students and women who were seeking employment. These students were hired during the summer months. This exposure to temporary employment in the corporate world enabled them to eventually obtain permanent positions at various Bell Laboratories' locations throughout the country.

My position as coordinator was enhanced by the supervisory expertise of the late Charles "Chuck" Evans. Mr. Evans gave me free reign to recruit and conduct my summer programs with a minimum amount of supervision from him. If it were not for his expertise in training me, however, I would not have been able to accomplish so much in this assignment.

For the next five years, I worked successfully with numerous college students. Not only was the Summer Research Program successful, but it also provided me with the opportunity to become acquainted with these students in such a way that I actually considered them my proteges. To this day, I have continued to follow the paths of some of these students, many whom continued to further their education by achieving doctorate degrees.

In 1984, the Bell System underwent major changes. As the result of a divestiture with the Bell System, a new company was formed, Bell Communications Research, Inc. This company was no longer affiliated with the Bell System. I transferred from Bell Laboratories, and subsequently joined the newly formed company. I accepted a position with this company as a secretarial supervisor. In addition to supervising secretaries, I was also involved in the training of new secretarial and clerical employees.

I remained in this position until 1988, when I finally decided to take early retirement from the corporate world. Shortly after my retirement, I began to get "itchy feet." In late 1989, I applied for volunteer service again with the United States Peace Corps. As before, I specified that I wanted to serve in an African country, and if at all possible, a French-speaking country.

As much as I tried for the French-speaking country, it was not to be. Seemingly, positions of this type were not available at the time I applied. But my desire to join the Peace Corps again was so strong that I finally accepted a teaching position in Sierra Leone, West Africa. Ironically, this was the country that I had previously visited in 1988 when I went on holiday to spend some time with my old friend, Ambassador Cynthia S. Perry.

On July 4, 1990, I was on my way again towards a new and challenging venture. This time, 41 volunteers were scheduled for Sierra Leone. We all met in Atlanta, Georgia, where we spent three and one-half days in orientation and briefing. We also received necessary immunization shots that were required for occupancy in that country.

At the time of the orientation, I thought the process had been carried out rather well by the Peace Corps staff and former Peace Corps volunteers. It was not until I arrived in Sierra Leone that I realized how weak the orientation had been, and how we had been so misinformed by these Peace Corps staff members who had conducted the orientation.

Sierra Leone had been portrayed to us in a different light than what it really was. We had not been told about the total lack of communication facilities in the country, nor how completely isolated we would be from contact with the United States most of the time. Nevertheless, with the exception of one volunteer who changed his mind, forty of us left for Sierra Leone on July 7, 1990.

We arrived in Sierra Leone on July 8, 1990, where we were met at the airport by a Peace Corps volunteer who was already serving in the country. After taking more than two hours to retrieve our luggage, we were finally whisked away by bus to our destination. There followed a four-hour arduous journey to our training site in the town of Panlap.

We reached Panlap about 2:00 am. The building grounds of the training site were sturdy and livable. We had water and electricity and inside toilets. During the training, however, the toilets were constantly clogged up and required service. We were housed two volunteers to a room. We had been instructed to bring our own linen and a few household articles. The beds provided were covered with old, damp mattresses, which, in many cases, were infested with bedbugs. It was obvious that the rooms had not been serviced or maintained for quite some time.

Now, bear in mind, we were the Peace Corps volunteers. We were assigned to a Third World country. Our mission was to teach, not only in areas of education, but also to teach the Sierra Leoneans good, clean health habits, how to maintain cleanliness, and how to prevent diseases. So here we were, in a site maintained by Peace Corps, but with all the elements of an unhealthy environment.

The next morning, we were aroused very early by our program director. We were informed that, after breakfast, we would be going to the village of Panlap to meet the chief of the village. It is a standard custom in Sierra Leone that when newcomers arrive at a village to spend any length of time, the first important step for them to take is to meet the chief of the village.

The chief's home was located about three or four miles from our training site. I'm not sure about the distance, but as we marched in the intense heat, it seemed like forever! We had formed a procession, and together with a small band, began our long journey to meet the chief. We literally danced our way to the village, and the small band of musicians was very rhythmic and colorful. As we marched along, many Sierra Leoneans on the road joined us, and soon we had a contingent of more than 200 people.

When we arrived at the village, we were greeted by the chief and members of his village council. Each volunteer was required to introduce him/her self and give their home state. A Sierra Leone language instructor served as interpreter for the chief and his council. Most of the members of the council were from the Themne tribe, and, except for the chief, spoke very little English.

After exchanging many pleasantries, we then departed and proceeded to make the long trek back to our training site. The march to the village will forever stay in my memory as a joyful moment of my return to Africa!

When we reached our site, we settled down and prepared to adjust to our surroundings. We had laundry facilities, outdoor clothes lines and buckets to do our own laundry if we wanted to. In my case, I elected to have one of the workers take care of my laundry for a small fee. This was my way of helping someone economically, the same as I had done in Kenya.

Kitchen and cooking facilities were also available. Our meals were prepared by Sierra Leoneans employed by Peace Corps. We ate from plastic dishes that were corroded from long wear. The Sierra Leoneans were not too adept in dishwashing, and the poor condition of the dishes did not help. Here the ingenuity of the Peace Corps volunteer was clearly displayed. After a short period of time at the training site, the volunteers began to assist in the dishwashing process, stressing to the Sierra Leoneans the mandatory use of hot water. The volunteers eventually persuaded the Peace Corps staff to get new dishes, and they continued to monitor the kitchen during our entire stay in Panlap

The diet for us volunteers consisted of Sierra Leone food for our main meal. This was a dish called "chop." It included rice and cassava, or rice and potato leaves, or rice and beans, and sometimes rice with a small amount of meat. The other two meals were so-called American dishes, such as spam, a macaroni mix, lots of cheese, and a few salads.

We became adjusted to the food, and in my case, the chop was more palatable than the American dishes, which were really bad. Clearly the Peace Corps staff did not have our dietary interests in mind when they planned our meals. Maybe because the Peace Corps staff did not have to eat this food, they ignored our dietary needs. The staff received food supplies by direct shipment from the United States, or they had shopping privileges at the United States commissary located in Sierra Leone. This was true not only for the Peace Corps staff members, but Americans who were assigned to the U.S. Embassy as well. Their imported food consisted of all the basic staples, plus chicken, meats, frozen vegetables, desserts, cookies, popcorn (occasionally the Peace Corps staff would throw some popcorn and/or cookies our way.) Nevertheless, in spite of the rigorous eight-week training period and poor diet, most of the volunteers hung in there and succeeded in overcoming the many obstacles that confronted them.

Krio

24

One of the main segments of the Peace Corps training at Panlap was the introduction of a language called Krio.

Now there are many ethnic groups in Sierra Leone, the two largest being the Mende people who occupy the northern and eastern provinces, and the Themne people of the southern and western provinces. These ethnic groups speak their respective languages, in addition to English and Krio. Illiteracy is about 85% in Sierra Leone, and many of the Sierra Leoneans speak no English at all. In place of English they speak Krio, which is a form of broken English.

Our language instructors were comprised of Mende, Themne, and a few other ethnic groups. They were well educated and had a good command of the English language. The Krio language was, to me, and to the Sierra Leone educators, a form of bad English. Peace Corps' reasoning was that we needed to learn Krio in order to communicate with the "bush" people, the illiterates, so to speak. I was a teacher in Sierra Leone, and in my contact with the schools, Krio was unacceptable. To the Sierra Leone educators this was just a method of perpetuating the illiteracy of the people. Teachers and students were not allowed to speak Krio on the school grounds. I found that, when communicating with vendors, children, young people and older people, it was just as easy to speak correct English slowly and they would understand, rather than sticking to the use of Krio. I felt that by presenting myself in this way, I was helping that person to learn correct English.

The languages of Mende and Themne were not introduced to us until a few days before the end of our training. When I did my bush area live-in, the family spoke Themne most of the time. With the exception of the father, and a few of the older children, the other family members were illiterate. Here are some examples of the Krio language:

(1) I bin kam = She came
     I de kam = She is coming
     I bin don kam = She had come
(2) Wetin dis? = What is this?
     Wetin dat? = What is that?
(3) Au di bodi? = How are you? (How is the body?)
(4) Wetin yu de du naya? = What do you do here?
     I de lan fo tok Krio = I learn to talk Krio
(5) Wetinda yu de lan to tok Krio? = Why do you learn to talk Krio?
     Bekos a want fo understand wetin pipul de token =
     Because I want to understand the way people talk

I could go on and on illustrating the Krio language, and what appears to be a complete distortion of the English language. Why, in heaven's name, couldn't Peace Corps at least have set up a program for teaching the basic ethnic languages, Mende and Themne, and just include Krio as an example of illiteracy, if even introducing it at all? Here was a country (one of the first countries) that had achieved independence more than 30 years ago, and Peace Corps was seemingly still impeding the progress of the people of Sierra Leone.

The administrative working staff at our Peace Corps office in Freetown was composed of all Sierra Leone employees, that is, the secretaries, accountants, nurses, and clerical personnel. They were literate and spoke good English. So why did the American Peace Corps staff, and also some of the Peace Corps volunteers, insist upon practicing their Krio on them? Instead of teaching them it appeared to me that they were really trying to keep the Sierra Leoneans from progressing.

When I arrived at my school in the village of Taiama, the students spoke English. Their ethnic origin was, in most cases, Themne. Our principal constantly reminded the teachers not to speak Krio to the students, to teach and converse in English. English was the instrument for educating the student, the instrument for future employment, and the universal instrument for progress of the people.

I spoke about the teaching of Krio to the Peace Corps program director. I pointed out to him, that I, as a black American, could not condone the teaching of Krio, since, in many respects, it resembled the bad dialect that I had been exposed to during my early years. It also symbolized a lot of the bad English that I hear being used today by many black Americans in the United States. Had I not pursued my education, and been taught by teachers who cared and understood, I would no doubt, have ended up still speaking a similar form of Krio, bad English.

To the white American Peace Corps staff and volunteers, learning Krio was fun, an anomaly, something to joke about. To me, as a black American, it was an insult, a disgrace, a tragedy. I realize that the Krio language is a part of the Sierra Leone culture, just as the negro dialect is a part of our black American culture. But for us, as volunteers, who, in a sense can be considered ambassadors of good will, I don't think perpetuating the use of Krio is the answer to our educational efforts. One may argue that I dwell on this use of Krio too harshly, but I don't think so.

One may say that teaching Krio to the volunteers was a means of economical assistance for the language instructors. These instructors were educated. They had a mastery of the English language, and their own cultural languages. They could just as easily adjusted to teaching us whatever language Peace Corps demanded. Progress cannot be made in the Third World countries if we continue to impede their chances for learning with the teaching of illiterate methods. Perhaps my bit of input will cause Peace Corps to consider changing some of their training methods in the future. Let us hope so.

The Krio language brings to mind the proposal to teach a language called "Ebonics" to black Americans in some areas of the United States. Ebonics is another form of bad English.

It is, in my opinion, another way to help to impede the progress of the black American.

As previously stated, the Sierra Leone instructors were highly educated. Many of them spoke other languages, in particular, French. In fact, the African seems to just have a natural capacity for speaking many languages, a skill that the average American does not have. During the course of my language training, I participated in private French tutoring from one of the instructors, Fred Ngaima. Also, when I began teaching in Taiama, I also engaged the services of another instructor for private French lessons. In both instances, I paid them a small fee for their services, a way of helping them economically. In this connection, I am forever grateful to Fred Ngaima for his patience, and for his friendship during my stay in Sierra Leone.

RAINETTE WITH FRED NGAIMA
LANGUAGE INSTRUCTOR

Family Live-In

25

Our eight-week training period also included a "live-in" experience similar to the one I had in Kenya, only this time the live-in was a bit more rugged and realistic. Each volunteer was placed in the home of a Sierra Leone family for three consecutive week-ends. During the week we returned to our training site for workshops. In most cases, the live-in conditions were fairly suitable. In one particular case, however, conditions at one live-in were so bad that the volunteer had to return to the training site and forego her live-in experience.

This particular volunteer, who at the time was my roommate, became ill as the result of the extremely poor and dangerous living conditions to which she was exposed. In her case, for some unknown reason, the Associate Peace Corps Director (APCD) kept insisting that she return to this family. The live-in conditions were seriously affecting her health, and she informed him that she could not return. Consequently, because of her refusal, this APCD sent her back to the United States. She was very upset about this decision and made an appeal to the Washington office. I learned later that this volunteer was given consideration, and was eventually sent to another assignment. This is one of the examples of complacency and incompetence that existed among some of the Peace Corps staff members. Later, I was to undergo a similar experience by this same APCD on my first bush assignment.

Although Peace Corps had previously made arrangements with the Sierra Leone families to have suitable housing for all the volunteers, in some cases things could just not be set up as planned due to the poor conditions under which some of the families were living. In my roommate's case, it was regrettable that the APCD could not seem to understand this. I was fortunate in that I was placed with a very fine family in the nearby town of Makeni. The family consisted of a husband with three wives and twenty children, the children being the combined offspring of all three wives. Polygamy is legal and acceptable in Sierra Leone and many other African countries, so this did not come as a surprise to me.

I was given a comfortable, clean room, that, I believe, belonged to the father. He had made preparations for my visit by painting the room and making it as comfortable for me as possible. During my stay, he slept in other less comfortable quarters. There was no electricity, no running water, and an outdoor latrine. Having been brought up in poverty myself, where electricity was absent and water often turned off, I could relate and adjust to these conditions. The outdoor latrine was clean, and when nature calls one does not hesitate to use whatever facilities are available. Whenever this call came late in the night, however, I used a small "potty" that I kept in my room. The fear of snakes and other dangers in the darkness overshadowed any extreme bravery I might have had to get me to go outside.

I felt a little uncomfortable at times, because I knew the family was going out of its way to make me as comfortable as possible. Their warmness and friendliness, however, made me put aside any misgivings I might have had. The families that housed us were financially compensated by Peace Corps. This was Peace Corps' way of helping the families economically, and, of course, the families were grateful for this assistance.

During the course of my live-in, I was drawn to one of the children, a 15-year old boy named Peter. I was impressed by his seemingly advanced learning skills, and his mastery of the English and French languages. In addition, he was also proficient in his ethnic languages. Peter had a warm personality, and we hit it off right from the start when we first met. He had attended school periodically, but due to lack of school fees and proper uniforms, he had been forced to discontinue school. While I was living in with his family, I committed myself to pay Peter's school fees for one year. I also took him shopping and purchased the required school uniforms and other items he needed. I could see the potential in Peter. My only regret is that future events in the country curtailed my continued contact with him.

PETER CONTEH
STUDENT

*WITH HOST FAMILY CHILDREN
IN MAKENI TOWN*

SIERRA LEONE "MAMA"
MAKING PALM OIL

WITH HOST FAMILY "MAMA"

The Bush

26

Prior to the end of our training in Panlap, we were given assignments at various sites where we would eventually be working and living. We were all scheduled for pre-visits to get a look at our living quarters and surroundings. I, along with three other volunteers, departed for our bush sites on September 1, 1990. Each of us was going to a different location, but we were traveling together by automobile and would be dropped off at our designated site.

We made arrangements at the local bus depot in Makeni for a car and a driver. When we took off, there were five of us volunteers and three other passengers squeezed into a regular 4-passenger vehicle. By the time we got to our first destination, there were twelve passengers in the car! Traveling in Africa by auto often reminds me of the little car I use to see at the Ringling Brothers Circus many years ago. Perhaps the reader can recall the sight. A tiny car circles around the arena and out comes about 20 or 30 people. I never could figure out how they all got into that tiny car.

Our vehicle was rickety, low to the ground, and sputtered during the entire trip. I'm talking about a nine-hour drive! The roads were pitted, rocky, and treacherous. I thought we would never make it, but finally, we reached our first stop at a town called Port Loko. By this time all our "extra" passengers had alighted along the way and only we volunteers remained. Two of the volunteers got off at Port Loko, leaving me for my next stop in the town of Mangei. This was another three-hour drive for me alone.

After another three hours, I finally arrived in Mangei. Arrangements had been made for me to stop in Mangei, stay overnight with Barbara, another Peace Corps volunteer already working there, then continue on the next day to my site, which was Mombolo. When I got to the volunteer's house, I was informed by a neighbor that the volunteer was in Freetown at the Peace Corps office. I had no key to the volunteer's house, so I had no place to stay. The driver had dropped me off and continued on with other passengers he had picked up on the way to Mangei. So here I was, stranded in Mangei, surrounded by strangers, many who spoke no English at all. I trudged back to the depot where I had been dropped off and proceeded to try to get a ride to Mombolo. The people of Mangei were friendly, and soon helped me to make transportation connections.

The ride to Mambolo was even more treacherous than my rides to Port Loko and Mangei. I was the only passenger this time. The road was gutted and so narrow that, at times, I thought the vehicle would surely topple over!

I finally arrived safely in Mombolo where I proceeded to get directions to the home of Mr. Kamara, who was the principal of the school where I would be teaching. I was greeted warmly when I arrived at Mr. Kamara's home. His family offered me dinner, and then he made arrangements for me to spend the night on the school grounds at the home of one of the teachers.

The following day, I met with Mr. Kamara for an interview and discussion of plans and living quarters. I had hoped to get living quarters on the school grounds, however, I was informed by Mr. Kamara that housing on the school grounds was not available for Peace

Corps volunteers. I later learned that this was not true, and that in the past some of the volunteers had lived on the school grounds. In fact, one white volunteer had moved out of the house where I was assigned and given more comfortable quarters on the school compound.

When the interview was over, Mr. Kamara drove me to the house that had been designated as a Peace Corps volunteer residence. The house was badly in need of interior cleaning and painting. There were a few large holes in the ceiling where tiles had come out and never replaced. There was a refrigerator and a stove, but these appliances were no longer working. These appliances had previously been provided by Peace Corps, but they had not been maintained properly by former Peace Corps volunteers. There was a three-stone stove outside the premises, so I imagined that I would have to make use of it for cooking purposes. Or, I could purchase one of the many gas burners that were common in the villages.

At the time I checked the house, I failed to check the toilet facilities, and I will never, to this day, understand why I did not do this, since toilet facilities are a very important factor in bush living. The house was similar to the house where I had stayed the night before, and I guess I just assumed that toilet facilities were the same. Later, I realized how careless I had been in not checking out this important factor.

Prior to leaving Mr. Kamara's home, I received word that Barbara had now returned to Mangei. So, before I left, Mr. Kamara made arrangements for me to catch a vehicle to Barbara's home in Mangei. Another bumpy and treacherous ride, but I finally arrived.

Barbara offered me lodging for the night, but by now I was anxious to get back to Freetown. After spending about two hours with her, I proceed on into town. Barbara accompanied me to the police station in Mangei, informing me that connections to Freetown might be better if I waited near the station. She returned home, and I assured her that I felt safe waiting alone by the station.

Within the next hour, two Asian gentlemen in a small van approached and offered me a ride as far as Port Loko, which I accepted. When I got settled in the back of the van I was surprised to see that my other passenger was a friendly goat! He gave me no trouble except for a "baa, baa" now and then.

The driver of the vehicle would not accept any money from me for the ride when we arrived in Port Loko. I noticed a sign on the van door indicating that they were connected with a missionary organization. I thanked them and went on my way to seek further transport to Freetown. After waiting about two hours, I finally managed to catch a lorry that was going to Freetown. As usual, it was very crowded, but I arrived safely. I get into Freetown about 11:00 pm that night. It was pitch dark, and there were very few people on the streets. We had been told during training that after our return from the site visits, we should go to Freetown and seek lodging at the Peace Corps hostel located there.

When I alighted from the lorry, I cautiously approached a young taxi driver. He agreed to take me to the hostel, however, he admonished me for being out so late, alone, since he said that the streets were very dangerous at night. When we arrived at the hostel he got out of his car and escorted me to the door. A real "brother."

When I arrived at the hostel, I was told that there were no more beds available. I was exhausted by now and could not believe this turn of events. The caretaker of the hostel, Mr. Dalton, made arrangements for me to sleep on the living room couch which was considered part of the sleeping quarters when all beds were taken. I didn't care where I slept, I just wanted to get some rest!

The next morning, I met several of the volunteers from my group who had also returned from their site visits. We exchanged views and stories about our travels and site accommodations, or lack of, so to speak. Needless to say, we had a lot to talk about.

The next three days, we were housed in a nearby hotel, the Paramount. Accommodations were modern and comfortable. It felt good to have electricity, hot water, and good meals, if only for a few days.

The next step, which was a momentous occasion, was our swearing-in ceremony. This took place at Town Hall in Freetown. Our language instructors, Peace Corps staff, and a few dignitaries participated in this event. We were now full-fledged Peace Corps volunteers!

Some of the volunteers returned to the hostel before leaving for their designated sites. I was fortunate in obtaining a room at a volunteer's residence in Freetown. This volunteer had been in Sierra Leone for more than a year, and her assignment was in Freetown. Her apartment was comfortable, even though it came with huge cockroaches the size of mice. This was common in the city of Freetown, but the luxury of having electricity and water overshadowed these daily visitors.

PEACE CORPS VOLUNTEERS
GLORIA BELLAMY AND ROBB

Negatives And Positives

27

Prior to leaving for our permanent sites, the volunteers who were in Teacher Education participated in a one-week practice teaching program at one of the secondary schools in the town of Makeni. This practice teaching was a first time event for most of the volunteers. There were ten volunteers. I was appalled to learn that, with the exception of two of these volunteers and myself, none of the others had any previous teaching or practice teaching experience before coming to Sierra Leone. Once again, as with the Kenya experience, here was Peace Corps serving up inexperienced, and in my opinion, non-qualified persons to teach the Africans, but they were white, and when it came to teaching the Africans this is all that mattered.

The secondary school, as were so many schools in Sierra Leone, was poorly equipped with worn out blackboards, old desks and benches, and no water or toilet facilities. We were transported back and forth to the school each day. At least we had the comfort of returning to our quarters at the training site. The students, however, usually spent all their time at the school with no food or use of toilet facilities.

The students were receptive to our teaching efforts. The classes went well, and most of the volunteers, even those with no previous experience, performed fairly well. The final day of our practice teaching we elected one of the volunteers to act as spokesperson for our farewell address. I felt a little annoyed and uncomfortable when this spokesperson referred to the students as "you people." Even here in Africa, my white constituents had not learned that this expression is an insult to blacks, be they black Americans or Africans.

I suppose I should say here that my resentment of various expressions used by the white volunteers was due to the fact that, as a black American, I felt a propinquity towards the African. When the volunteers called the person working for them "house-boy" or "house-girl" this offended me, although this had been common usage by the Europeans when they controlled Sierra Leone and other African countries. When I overheard one of the white volunteers say, "I'm glad I wasn't born black," this upset me. Many times the white volunteers voiced their sentiments and opinions about the African, opinions that I considered unfavorable. Perhaps these volunteers believed that I, being an American, felt the same way they did. In no way was this true. I was an American, but I was also black and of African descent. These were my "brothers" and "sisters," and I considered them a part of my heritage.

I suppose that, having worked for the federal government for more than 20 years, I should have been accustomed to the bureaucratic methods and procedures that I witnessed in Sierra Leone. My experiences in Kenya with the Peace Corps staff had been relatively stable and well organized, so I was not quite prepared for the differences that occurred in Sierra Leone.

Some of the volunteers whom I came in contact with seemed to spend a lot of time in Freetown attending personal meetings, compiling a nonsensical newsletter, shopping at "junk" stores, and just hanging around the Peace Corps office doing nothing. I could never understand how they could be doing a good job on their assignments when they spent so much time in Freetown.

The "junk" stores were clothing outlets that, in many cases, had been set up from clothing and supplies originally intended as donations for the poor Africans. These donations were often confiscated and sold, thus depriving the people of the country from receiving them. The most frequent customers were usually expatriates, Peace Corps volunteers, and a few Africans who could afford the prices.

The Peace Corps staff in Sierra Leone seemed to lean more towards the welfare and comfort of the volunteer, rather than to the interest and concerns of the Sierra Leoneans. They even went so far as to give a big "bash" each year for the volunteers who had completed their two years of service. This involved a huge, expensive party at a local hotel. Why it was necessary to throw a party for the volunteers who had come to the country, supposedly to sacrifice and help the Africans, I'll never understand. I often wondered if Washington was aware of this extravagance.

On the positive side, I would like to mention a couple of volunteers whom I came in contact with and whom I considered dedicated to their assignments in Sierra Leone. One of these was David O'Neil, who was nearing completion of his Peace Corps assignment. He had been working on viable projects during his venture, enough to "make a difference." Until the very last day of his assignment, he was still working with the American Embassy, trying to get financial assistance for a special project. He succeeded in doing so before he left.

Another volunteer, John Tuck, also deserves mentioning. John was in the original group of 40 that came over to Sierra Leone. Before we had to leave the country, John's project was well underway. I was impressed by the fact that John gave credit for his successful project to the Sierra Leoneans he had been helping, and not to himself. He had been training them, and when they did well, he gave them credit for their accomplishments. John was one of the more mature volunteers, and perhaps this accounted for his positive attitude and success.

I must also give credit and accolades to one of the more competent Peace Corps staff members, Dr. C. Wall. He extended himself in many ways. In addition to serving our medical needs, he also went out of his way to make us comfortable in the new and strange environment that surrounded us in Sierra Leone. During our eight-week training period, he religiously came to the training center and gave us extensive lectures on health practices and other safety measures. Dr. Wall always welcomed volunteers to his home, and particularly, when the crisis in Sierra Leone was beginning, he was there to lend his support.

Another positive factor was the advent of Mr. W. Freer, a new Peace Corps Director. When we first arrived in Sierra Leone, the Peace Corps Director in the country at the time was nearing completion of his assignment, so we did not have very much contact with him. As the new incoming director, Mr. Freer did his best, and, considering the ineptness of some of the APCDs he had reporting to him, I don't think he should be held accountable for their shortcomings. He was extremely helpful and considerate when it became necessary for me and other volunteers to leave Sierra Leone due to the civil unrest that was taking place in the country.

Back To The Bush

28

In early September, I left for my permanent site in Mambolo. We departed from Freetown at 8:30 in the morning. There were two other volunteers who were also going to their sites, and our trips had been combined.

After a two-hour drive, one volunteer was dropped at his site. I was supposed to be the next drop-off, but the driver got lost and missed my drop-off point. Consequently, he proceeded on to the other volunteer's site, about a three-hour drive. Then we tried to find the way back to my site. After much struggling and strenuous travel through a torrential rainstorm and very treacherous roads, we finally arrived in Mambolo.

By now it was 8:00 pm. When we reached the principal's house, he gave me my key and directed the driver to take me to my house. When I arrived a small lantern was burning, the place had been painted and spruced up a bit, and was quite clean. The driver rested for a short time, then departed.

Feeling exhausted and sort of apprehensive, I rested on the couch that evening, deciding to check out other facilities the next day. I had no water, except for what I had in a small flask; however, this did not seem important at the time since I was just so very exhausted. I knew the next day someone would come to fetch water and do other chores for me.

There was another house next to mine, similar in appearance to my house. The following morning I went to meet my new neighbor. She was a young black American student who was going to work at the school where I was assigned. She was in a student exchange program. While checking out our living quarters, we discovered that the toilet facilities were adjoining the two houses and we would be sharing them. This student, Myra, had not checked out the toilet facilities prior to her permanent arrival either, so together we went to check them out.

We were quite disturbed to discover the toilet facilities were located outside our houses in another building. There was a crosswalk outside and we had to go through a small compound where other families were housed in order to reach the toilet.

We located our key, entered the toilet area, only to be greeted by huge spiders, the largest I had ever seen since my time in Africa! We immediately ran from the building, and, after getting our nerves together, entered again, only this time more cautiously. Stagnant, infested water and toilet waste filled the toilet bowl. When we tried to flush the toilet several times, it became apparent that the plumbing did not work. The area surrounding us was filthy.

Feeling a bit dismayed, we returned to our respective houses.

That evening I had no choice but to relieve myself as best that I could in one of the water buckets I had brought with me. Probably the strenuous trip, the excitement, and other factors attributed to a severe case of diarrhea because I was up all night using my bucket.

We reported the toilet problems to one of the principal's workers the next day. We were told that a plumber would soon arrive. I had also been told that someone would come to assist me with making an outside fire for cooking, and that he would also fetch water from the well which was about a mile from my house.

I waited for the plumber all day, but he did not show up, nor did the worker come to bring me water, nor did I hear from the principal again. That night I had to rely on my bucket again. By now, it was beginning to fill up. I was beginning to get hungry but I had no food. I had brought some cookies with me, so this was my meal for the night, and also the next few days.

After two days of waiting, unable to use the toilet, no water, no cooking facilities, and no word from the principal, I decided to pack my bags, leave Mambolo, and return to Freetown.

I contacted my neighbor, Myra, and she, too, was disturbed about our situation. She planned to go to the school later on that day, and said she would try to reach someone from her organization. I asked her to hold my luggage and utilities while I returned to Freetown. I gave her a letter for the principal in which I expressed my concerns and my reason for being unable to stay in Mambolo. I later learned that Myra stayed in Mambolo only a day or two after I left. She gave my luggage to the principal and departed for another assignment in the city of Bo.

I was disturbed and more than disappointed with what had occurred in Mambolo. By this time, my bout with the bucket had left me weak, and, in fact, I sensed that I had already lost a few pounds. Weight loss in Sierra Leone tends to be common among Peace Corps volunteers, and sometimes they have to be sent back to the states because of this. Rather than endanger my health any further, I departed early that morning and trudged on down by the river, looking for transportation to Freetown.

After a wait of about two hours by the river, I caught a driver going to Port Loko. When I arrived in Port Loko, the only vehicle available going to Freetown was a large lorry, carrying about 60 people. I had no choice. It was getting late and it was a long journey from Port Loko to Freetown. So I decided to climb aboard the lorry, and off we went!

By now, I had become use to various means of transportation, but this lorry ride was a real trip! As we traveled along, passengers came and went. For every one that got off, two or three more got on. They were carrying huge sacks of rice, potatoes, greens, and even huge tanks filled with palm oil. At various intervals we stopped. Road vendors greeted us with food for sale, oranges, sweets, and chop. It was almost like a roadside gathering! People got off, bought food, sat around the area eating and greeting one another; then they would climb back on the lorry, with a few more passengers joining us.

All along the way to Freetown, the drive continued to stop for passengers, some still dragging huge drums of palm oil. In addition, the driver allowed passengers to load large containers of kerosene on top of the lorry. This, in itself, was a real danger. Luckily we did not have an accident along the way although we hit many bumpy roads. I was afraid that some of the kerosene containers would spill over, but they never did.

By the time we reached Freetown, the original count of 60 passengers had increased to almost 100! We were packed like sardines, men, women, children, and many mothers carrying infants on their backs. There were also mattresses, live chickens, more drums of palm oil, and me!

We reached Freetown about 11:00 pm that night. I got a taxi to the hostel, found a cot to sleep on, and so to bed. Whew! What a day it had been!

The following day I attempted to reach my APCD, but he was upcountry visiting some of the sites at the time. It wasn't until a few days later that I was able to meet with him and tell him about the episode in Mambolo. He was less than understanding. He told me that I should have gone outside that night when I noted the condition of the toilet, and dug a pit latrine. Outside, in the middle of bush territory! The lack of food and water did not seem to phase him in the least. He just shrugged his shoulders and did not appear to be the least bit interested in my plight.

My APCD insisted that I return to Mambolo and give it another try. By now, however, I was thoroughly disgusted with his attitude. This was the same APCD who had mistreated my roommate in Panlap, causing her to be sent home. I concluded by now that he was not only disinterested, but, to put it mildly, incompetent in his role as an APCD. Ironically, he seemed to ignore and overlook the conduct of many other volunteers, who blatantly disregarded their assignments and did nothing but linger around the Peace Corps office all day.

I informed my APCD that, due to the unsafe and unsanitary conditions in Mambolo, I would not return to that site. He finally made arrangements for me to go back to Mambolo and collect my luggage. After doing this, I returned to Freetown for another assignment. In the meantime, no other volunteer was ever asked to replace me in Mambolo.

I remained at the Peace Corps hostel for approximately two weeks, waiting for another assignment. While at the hostel, I noticed that many of the volunteers seemed to be more or less vacationing. I learned that some had been in Sierra Leone for more than a year, still waiting to be assigned. They didn't really seem to care whether they were given a site or not. They were receiving their allowance so not having an assignment did not present a problem to them. Many of them had the same APCD as I, but he turned his head the other way where they were concerned. He did not insist that they be sent anywhere.

I was beginning to wonder why we were here in Sierra Leone. This was one of the first countries that Peace Corps had entered more than thirty years ago, yet nowhere could I see any noticeable signs of achievements or accomplishments. No wonder Peace Corps in Sierra Leone was often referred to as Peace "Corpse."

I will say this, however, that during our swearing-in ceremonies, one of the Sierra Leone language instructors stated that he had been taught and inspired by Peace Corps volunteers many years ago when they first came to Sierra Leone. This was during the 60s and 70s when there was an abundance of dedicated and conscientious volunteers. Over the years, however, somewhere along the way, the American Peace Corps staff members in Sierra Leone were becoming mediocre, and consequently, the volunteers were also becoming mediocre. To add to this sad state, Sierra Leone, itself, was beginning to crumble as a country.

Taiama

29

In late September, I was offered another Peace Corps assignment in the village of Taiama, located in the southern province of Sierra Leone. Subsequently, I visited Taiama and was given a tour of the school and my housing accommodations. This time I checked the toilet facilities. No running water, of course, but an inside toilet that worked by pouring water down the tank. Shades of my depression days! This I could live with.

I moved to Taiama in October and assumed my duties as typing teacher at the Taiama Secondary School. My house was spacious and in need of inside painting, but it was livable. By now I had observed that in all of Sierra Leone, painting was not a top priority. Buildings and edifices, although well constructed, had not been properly maintained or painted for 20 years or more.

The Taiama school and the surrounding buildings had probably once been very beautiful. But for some reason the areas had deteriorated beyond description. The school buildings were constructed of brick, with modern jalousie windows. Boarding accommodations were once available at the school, but these buildings were now empty. Even the house where I lived had the appearance of having once been very beautiful. It was of brick construction, had large, spacious rooms, a modern toilet and electrical outlets. Now there was no plumbing, cement floors were corroded, and walls were actually gray due to lack of painting for many, many years. What had happened to this once beautiful village? What had happened to most of Sierra Leone? It was sad and very depressing. A once beautiful country had now almost become a picture of ancient ruins.

The principal of the school, Mr. Thomas Senessie, was friendly and pleasant. He had arranged for his nephew, Christian, who was employed at the school, to work for me part time. Christian would take care of fetching water, making the outside kitchen fire, washing and ironing, running errands, and other miscellaneous chores. I paid Christian out of my living allowance. We did not have to hire workers unless we wanted to, but, once again, it was my way of helping one more African.

The kitchens for cooking in the villages are usually located outside the house in a hut-type building. Each day Christian made a fire for me to boil water and do my cooking. The water had to be boiled in accordance with Peace Corps health instructions. We had been provided with a filtering device whereby, after boiling the water, we put it through this filtering process before using. The Sierra Leoneans do not boil their water, thus it was quite a chore for Christian to get use to this particular ritual every day. The high rate of cholera and many other diseases in Sierra Leone and other African countries can be attributed to contaminated water.

Before moving to our living quarters in Sierra Leone, we had been told by Peace Corps that they would pay for various needs, such as paint supplies. I contacted the Peace Corps office to get funds for painting the interior of my house. Mr. Senessie had given me an estimate of the amount of paint I would need and also provided his school painter to do the work for me. I submitted a bill for approximately $250 (American dollars) to cover the cost. My APCD (the same one who had given me such a bad time about my assignment in Mambolo) refused to approve the entire amount, even though I gave him an itemized receipt. He approved $150.00 and I had to pay the balance of $100 out of my living allowance. Some volunteers were able to get money for all their needs, but others, like myself, were less fortunate. The reason for this was never clear to me.

Anxious to get adjusted and settled in my new surroundings, I did not question this obvious double standard. Problems similar to this often came up between me and my APCD during my stay in Sierra Leone, nevertheless, I learned to cope with them. I was in Sierra Leone to work, help, and make a difference, so I did not make a big issue of these inconsistencies that took place. Whenever I did approach him with questions or concerns, he made a point of avoiding the issue. I chalked it up to his incompetence, rather than using the old alibi of racism, and let it go at that.

Finally, after two weeks and three coats of paint (it could have used five), my house was painted. I had purchased some cotton material from the nearby town of Bo, and managed to sew the material together as curtains for the large windows. The principal arranged for his carpenter to come and install screening at all the windows to keep the hornets, mosquitoes, and other bugs out.

I had purchased a kerosene stove to do away with the outside cooking which had become quite a task for me. The stove did not work properly most of the time, so I was soon back outside struggling with the outdoor "three-stone" fire. This consisted of three large stones placed together, then covered with branches, sprinkled with kerosene, and ignited. It may sound like our outdoor barbecue style of cooking back in the states, but for some reason I could not get the hang of it. Most of the time I had to rely on Christian to come to my rescue and keep the fire going.

My days at Taiama eventually took on a steady routine. Up at 6:30 am; took my bucket bath, dressed and boiled water for tea. Breakfast consisted of tea, bread and an orange or banana. I bought fresh bread from my next-door neighbor who was a teacher at the school. This bread baking was an extra source of income for him. While doing all of this, I listened to the BBC broadcasting station on my battery-operated radio. Oh, one other ritual I had to go through before leaving for school was to shake out the bat drippings from my clothes closet every morning. More about my bat experiences later. Then off to school which was about a five-minute walk from my house.

Classes started at 7:45 am. The first 15 minutes were devoted to prayer, roll call, and announcements. Sometimes after the announcements, certain students were called forward to take punishment. Punishment consisted of "flogging" by a teacher or the principal. The student being punished may have been late for classes, may have been insolent, may have failed to perform a certain task, or may not have been prepared for reciting a prayer before classes began. In any case, the student was put before the entire class to receive the flogging, usually three strokes, but sometimes a few more if the misconduct warranted it.

It was the first time I had ever witnessed flogging, and it was one custom that I never got used to. On second thought, however, maybe this wasn't such a bad idea in order to maintain discipline within the school. I'm sure our students in the United States, if the law allowed it, could use a little of this flogging now and then to solve our discipline problems.

I had previously toured the school on my initial visit to Taiama, but I had not been given a thorough inside view of all the classrooms. When I began working at the school I was able to get a closer look at the surroundings. I was astonished at the condition of the classrooms. Old, worn out desks and chairs, classroom walls in need of plastering, and blackboards no longer black. The black had worn off almost completely and chalk writing was barely legible to the students. Since there was no electricity, the classrooms had very poor lighting. Fortunately, the large glass windows, or no window panes at all, provided a source of light.

There were no toilet facilities for the students, and no water. The students were in school from 7:45 am to 2:00 or 3:00 pm each day. Nearby bushes were used for their toilet needs. Washing of hands was often done in nearby rain barrels when they were full. At other times, they were unable to wash their hands at all. The teaching staff had use of a small toilet located next to the staff room. Drinking water was also provided in a large container. A hand dipper was used to pour this water into plastic cups. I did not drink this water because it had not been boiled, and always waited until I returned home after class to get drinking water.

There was no classroom available for my typing class. I was able to make use of the Library building for my classes. The typewriters had been donated to the school by a former Peace Corps volunteer. They were not new, but they were workable. They were not nearly as bad as the machines that Peace Corps had donated to my Kenya secretarial school.

The typewriters were manual, and from time to time we had to make a few adjustments to get the ribbons to reverse automatically. The machines were placed on the library tables since there were no desks available, and we used regular hard back library chairs. This was not the best setting for correct typewriting posture, but we had no choice.

Our classes soon got underway. I had a small class of 15 students. Due to the cramped quarters, my classes were divided into three sessions. Eventually everything began to run smoothly, and the typewriters were holding up rather well. We had 12 machines, but only 9 were usable. With the three sessions, there were always enough machines to work with.

We were now almost two months into our school work. One morning, in late November, I went to my library classroom as usual.

Upon entering the classroom, I noticed that two typewriters were missing from their usual places on the table. I made inquiries at the principal's office, thinking that perhaps someone had borrowed them. After a few inquiries, it became clear to all of us that the typewriters had been stolen! Two of our best machines! Our examinations were scheduled within a few days. (Shades of Kenya secretarial school!)

That afternoon, I , the principal, and the library teacher had to go to the local police station, a distance of about a mile from the school. We had to report the incident and give individual statements to the police. This took about three hours. Then we were released.

Later, the police came to the school and there was much speculation as to how the thieves had entered the library, which had been locked. It was finally concluded that they had entered through some very high windows located at one end of the building. This was an amazing feat since the windows were extremely high. However, this seemed to be the only way they could have gotten in. It wasn't until I returned to the states the following year that I learned the thieves had been caught, but the typewriters were never recovered.

It was quite a struggle to continue on with our classes, especially since our best typewriters had been stolen, but we managed. The students sat for their first typing examinations, similar to the standard typing examinations that are given in the states and not the East African examinations that were given in Kenya. It would be a while before these students could sit for East African examinations since we did not yet have suitable machines.

After completion of the typing examinations, I had planned to introduce shorthand to the students the following semester. These plans were cancelled within a few months because of the civil unrest that was beginning to sweep the country of Sierra Leone.

Bush Life In Taiama

30

After a few months with me, Christian had to give up his part time work at my house because demands at the school required more of his time. Mr. Bah recommended one of his students, Dominic Bangura, to assist me. I was very pleased with Dominic's work, and we soon became good friends. Dominic also had school fee problems since he came from a very poor family. When I returned to the United States, I made arrangements through Mr. Senessie to pay for Dominic's education until he completed secondary school. These arrangements were to change drastically when the trouble in Sierra Leone became more serious.

As time passed, I began to love my little village. The life style was rather rugged, but it was peaceful and tranquil. Things were going fairly well at the school. The school, like my school in Kenya, had a sports program which lasted for one week. It was a great event in Taiama village; a time of joy and excitement. The sports events were held in a large field adjacent to the school. The students in Taiama were also tremendous athletes like those in Kenya. Once again, I witnessed some terrific athletes and sports events.

On Sundays, I attended the nearby Methodist church. Even though the songs were sung in Themne, the tunes were familiar since they were the same as those sung in the Methodist and Episcopal churches in the

United States. The lessons and scripture were read in English, so I had no difficulty in following them. I was even asked to read one Sunday and considered this an honor.

On Easter morning there was a 5:00 a.m. baptismal service for adults down by the river. Later, at the regular church service, infants and small children were baptized. It was a moving sight to witness! The sole portrait in the church is a large mural depicting a black Christ standing with Peter and the fishermen. This portrait had been donated to the church many years ago.

As previously mentioned, electrical outlets were still in most of the houses and schools in Taiama. There was a small generator in an area near my house. During the Christmas holidays, and on very special occasions, the principal turned on the power and we had electricity. These were exciting times, and the students were allowed to have disco at the school when electricity was available. I might add here that the discos were the same as those in the states, loud and thumping.

Having made friends with many of the people in my village, it was common for me to open my door some mornings and receive young children. They had been sent by their parents to bring me fruit, usually oranges and bananas. Although they themselves may have had a sparse diet of rice and cassava leaves, they still had enough to share something with me. It saddens me, even now, to think that within a few months this new happiness and contentment that I had found would soon be over.

During the next few months, as I settled down in Taiama, I encountered a few strange events that took place. I would like to relate a few of them at this time.

As was the custom in Taiama, I slept with a mosquito net over my bed at all times. The mosquitoes were not such a menace, but spiders were a problem. Every afternoon when I came home from school, I would be met by large black spiders, some the size of a small alarm clock. They were all over the place, the bedroom, kitchen, living room walls and the toilet. The insect repellent I used was useless. The more I sprayed, the more spiders came out!

Usually, when the spray can emptied, I grabbed the broom, a makeshift object made of branches and pounded away! I became an expert at killing spiders before I left Sierra Leone. One time I almost overlooked a huge spider just before sitting on the toilet. After that, I always inspected before sitting. Roaches were not too bad; nothing compared to those huge monsters I met in Freetown. In fact, after a few sprays, they disappeared completely.

Now I will discuss the "noises" in my house. Every night, upon retiring, I would hear these creaky, creaky noises. My bedroom door was locked. The principal had even provided me with a security guard who sat outside my bedroom window every night. But there were these noises that sounded like someone was trying to break in my house. I would get out of bed, light my bedside candle, or use my flashlight, and go into the living room. But there would be nothing. When I got up every morning, all would be quiet and the watchman was gone. I would even come home from school in the late afternoon, sit in my living room, and wait for the noises. There would be none, until after I retired for the night, then the noises would begin again.

One day, I happened to mention these noises to one of the teachers. He started laughing, then gave me an explanation for the noises. The roof of my house was made of zinc. Zinc is ductile. The extreme heat of the day, coupled with the cooling in the evening, causes the roof to contract, thus the noises. This was something I had to live with, but I never really got used to those noises in the night!

This was not the end of the mysterious noises in my house, however. One night I thought I heard some squealing sounds like a mouse. Now what was this all about? I got up, lit my candle again, looked around my bedroom and the living room, but nothing was there. Later that week, while conversing with a missionary nurse who lived nearby, I mentioned the squealing. She informed me that my house was full of bats! This was not unusual, she said, since Taiama was known for its bats. She said they were probably in the eaves of my house. She also said that they were harmless. The bats were known to settle in houses, leave at night, then return early in the morning.

One evening, shortly after this conversation with the missionary, I heard a swishing noise, like a heavy wind blowing, outside my house. It only lasted for a few seconds. I began to listen for this sound every evening. It usually occurred a little after 7:00 pm, just before I retired. A few nights later, after hearing this sound again, I looked out of my bedroom window. Lo and behold! I saw hundreds of bats coming out from the roof of my house! Swish! Swish! And then they were gone! I quickly went to bed, shaken up, to say the least!

Now in the morning, I became aware of noises in my bathroom ceiling. When I opened the toilet door each morning, I would hear a scurrying sound overhead. I concluded that it was the bats. They were sleeping after being out all night. When they heard the bathroom door open, they awoke and started scurrying around. When I kept still, they quieted down.

This soon became a daily routine. In the evening, at exactly 7:20 pm, not one minute earlier or one minute later, the bats would leave my house in swarms. I never heard them when they returned, but like clockwork, when I opened the toilet door in the morning, they started scurrying around. Just as I was becoming use to the "bats in my belfry," I opened the bathroom door one morning and, guess what? There was this brown thing, squirming in my bathtub, struggling to get out. A bat! I ran out of the house, called Mr. Bah, my neighbor, and he hurried over. Naturally, he laughed at my behavior, calmly picked up the bat and threw it in the field. From then on I opened the bathroom door more cautiously. During my stay in Taiama, a few more bats squeezed through the rafters in the ceiling and landed in my bathtub. In each case, Mr. Bah removed them for me.

I even became accustomed to the bats. One evening, with Christian still at the house, I videotaped the bats leaving my house. One flew into my living room, but with the help of Christian, it was caught and also videotaped. As I became more aware of the bats, I noticed that they were leaving various other houses around me, at the same time, 7:20 pm every evening. Thousands of them! The bats of Taiama. What a phenomenon!

The next little bit of excitement at my home, occurred one day when I was sitting outside, correcting school papers and listening to radio music. I happened to glance down, momentarily, and saw a long, brown snake looking up at me! I arose slowly, but carefully, moved away from the house and then began to run! By this time, Mr. Bah had noticed me running and quickly came over with a large stick. By the time he arrived, the snake had sidled away, disappearing somewhere in the bushes. From that time on, I corrected my school papers inside my house.

One other event in my Taiama village life bothered me considerably. We had no regular site for dumping trash or garbage. Consequently, I had to throw the garbage away in a nearby field not too far from my house. I was surprised and perturbed one day when I noticed that children were rummaging through the garbage, looking for food. I also noticed that my night security guard often went through the garbage looking for leftovers. I never adjusted to these actions, but I realized more and more that hunger was still a serious factor in this poverty stricken country.

MR. THOMAS N,B, SENESSIE, PRINCIPAL

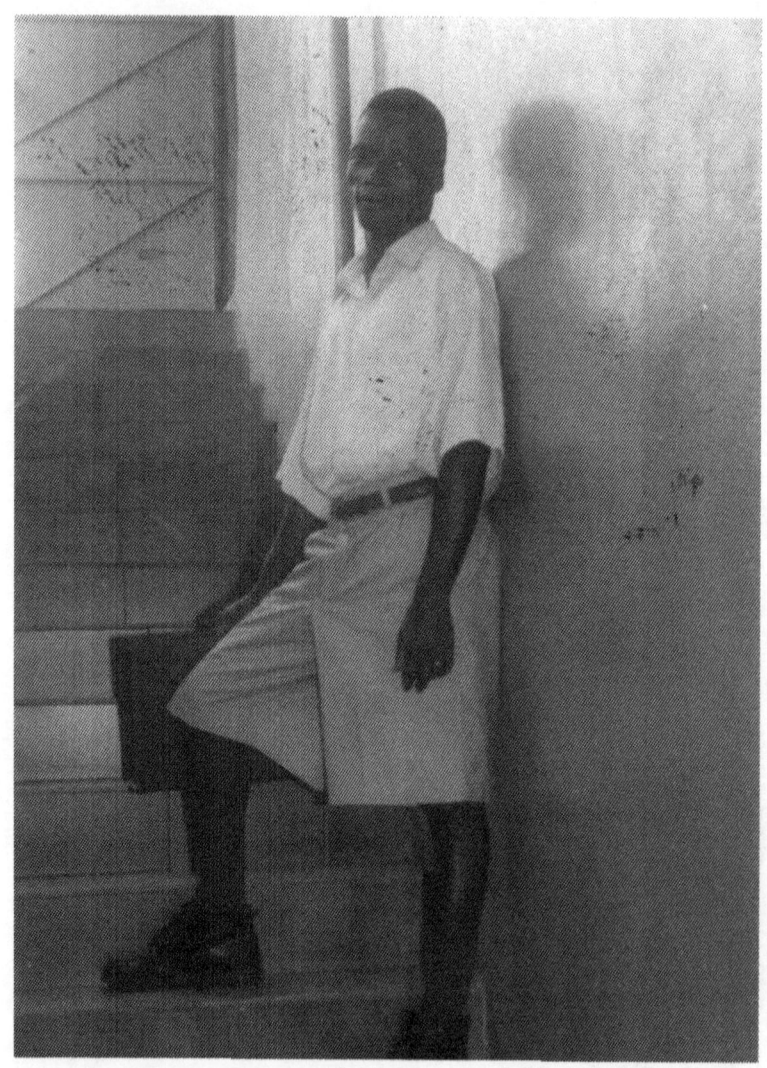

DOMINIC BANGURA, STUDENT–1996

MR. SENESSIE'S CHILDREN

TAIAMA NEIGHBORHOOD CHILDREN

Deja Vu

31

In March of 1991, the political situation in Sierra Leone became critical. The nearby country of Liberia was engaged in serious fighting. Thousands of civilians had been killed. Liberian refugees were pouring into Sierra Leone. Rumors were rampant about a possible invasion of Sierra Leone. And then there began to appear ominous headlines in the local newspapers: "War, It's Time We Contain Taylor And His Rebels;" "Rebels Attack But Army Moves;" "Sierra Leone Helping the Rebels;" "Allies Free Koindu? 250 Rebels Killed;" These frightening headlines seemed similar to those I had seen in Tehran, Iran. Only this time it was Sierra Leone. To me it was deja-vu!

We continued on with our studies at the school, but day by day we were constantly listening to reports on the radio. The village people were making less and less trips to Freetown, afraid that something chaotic might happen while they were on the road. I began to prepare for my 10-day Easter holiday since school would be closed. I planned to spend most of the holiday in Freetown. As I packed my duffel bag, I had a premonition that perhaps I would not be returning to Taiama. The news was getting worse every day. I decided to pack a second duffel bag and leave it at my house in Taiama. In this bag I placed all my other personal belongings in the event I did return to Taiama if only to pick up these other articles.

The morning of my departure for Freetown, Mr. Bah came to escort me to the bus depot. It was pitch dark at 4:30 a.m., but I had a large flashlight to guide us down the road. The distance to the depot was a little over a mile. The bus to Freetown was scheduled to leave at 6:00 a.m.

Mr. Bah had brought his portable radio along, since by now, everyone was listening to as much news as they could concerning the Liberian/Sierra Leone situation. As we sat by the road waiting for the bus, we heard over the French Guinea broadcast that rebel Liberian forces were entering the border of Sierra Leone and that fighting had erupted. Villagers were being warned to remain at home. Guinean occupants of Sierra Leone were being told to return to Guinea, another bordering country.

Before boarding the bus, I gave Mr. Bah my flashlight to use while I was away in Freetown. He quietly left me at the depot. As I watched him gradually fade out of sight, I had this sad feeling that possibly I would not be returning to Taiama, and would never see him again. Mr. Bah had been very kind, helping me to settle in and adjust to the village life style. I knew I would miss him very much.

For the first time, since traveling to and from Freetown, I experienced my first police check as we entered other areas. All passengers on the bus had to alight, show their identification, and then we were allowed to board the bus again. This practice of police checks continued throughout my remaining days in Sierra Leone.

When I arrived at the office in Freetown, I was greeted with the news that Peace Corps was in the process of evacuating some of the volunteers who were stationed at various bush sites and would be bringing them back to Freetown. The situation in Sierra Leone was now very serious. Had I not already been on my way to Freetown, Peace Corps personnel would have eventually come to Taiama to collect me from my village.

By the end of the week, the Peace Corps hostel was full. Some volunteers had been placed in private homes of staff members. Some were staying with volunteers who were already assigned to the Freetown area.

On April 29, 1991, all Peace Corps volunteers were requested to assemble at the American Embassy for a special meeting. The United States Ambassador greeted us and proceeded to calm our fears about the critical situation in Freetown. Most of the volunteers, particularly those in the southern part of the country, like myself, were told that they would not be returning to their sites. Those in the northern part were given the choice of returning to their sites since the situation in that part of the country did not appear to be critical. The information given to us by the ambassador was so vague that I left the meeting feeling rather confused and uneasy. There still seemed to be an air of uncertainty about just how serious the situation was in Sierra Leone. As we left the embassy, I could not help but notice the long lines of Sierra Leoneans who were waiting to be processed for permits to leave the country.

Within less than a week after the meeting at the embassy, my name was listed as one of those from the southern area who could return to their village. The village of Taiama is located close to Bo, a nearby city where I often traveled to do my grocery shopping. Bo had been cited as one of the danger zones during this civil unrest. When I approached my APCD and inquired about the danger of returning and being so close to Bo, he shrugged his shoulders (as usual) and said, "You can return to Taiama, but you can't go to Bo and shop. If anything serious happens, you are on a nearby travel road. It's highly probable that Peace Corps would come and get you out in time."

Now the road from Freetown to Taiama takes about four to five hours during peaceful times. With the police check now in effect, the travel time had almost doubled. The term "highly probable" did not sound like a very promising rescue in case of trouble. From my previous experience in Iran, I began to have serious doubts about remaining in Sierra Leone, let alone returning to my site. I had the feeling that no one really seemed to know what was actually going on.

Even though I had been told that I could return to Taiama, I hesitated. My principal had not contacted me. He often traveled to Freetown, but because of the dangerous situation now going on, he had been forced to cancel his travel plans. So how did my APCD expect me to return to Taiama if my principal couldn't even make it to Freetown?

By now, most of us volunteers were just sitting around the Peace Corps office waiting for news about our individual sites and getting updates about the situation in Sierra Leone. One day, while sitting in the lounge, we received some startling news about a volunteer who had been living in Sierra Leone for a number of years. She had extended her initial assignment several times. During this period, she had married a Sierra Leonean and was living in a small village in the southern province. She had just returned from home leave in the states, and had checked into the Peace Corps office before returning to her village.

When she was in the states, preparing for her return trip to Sierra Leone, Peace Corps, Washington, had not notified her of the trouble that was taking place in Sierra Leone. Nor did anyone from the Sierra Leone Peace Corps office contact her before she left the states. She was totally unaware of the serious situation that was occurring, so she returned to Sierra Leone.

While sitting in the lounge, she was called to the office and told that her husband had been a victim of a rebel infiltration in her village, and that he had been killed. As one can well imagine, the next 24 hours were very traumatic and stressful for her. She was told that she could not return to her village, even though her husband was dead, and even though she had dependent children back in the village. Within a day or so, this volunteer was sent back to the states, permanently, without having been allowed to contact anyone in her village before she left. I don't know if the fact that this was a white volunteer married to a Sierra Leonean had anything to do with this decision. To this day, I do not know whatever transpired concerning the fate of her children.

Conditions at the Peace Corps hostel were becoming tense and uncomfortable. Communal living among some of the volunteers was at a high peak. Volunteers were beginning to worry, and tempers were short. Peace Corps had finally told us that those who wanted to could return to the United States. Some of the volunteers were disappointed and reluctant to return home, but the bureaucracy and uncertainty that prevailed in the Peace Corps office made it necessary for many of us to decide to leave.

Mr. Freer, our Peace Corps Director, along with office personnel, participated in making travel arrangements for many of the volunteers who were leaving. Every day a contingent of volunteers could be seen leaving for the airport. This was not an evacuation like I experienced in Iran, but it was the beginning of a complete exodus by the American Peace Corps.

Sorrowful Ending

32

In May, 1991, I returned to the United States. I was relieved that I had escaped from Sierra Leone safe and sound, but I was extremely disappointed that this second Peace Corps venture had ended so traumatically.

In the Spring of 1992, more headlines: "U. S. States Evacuates 100 Americans from Coup-torn Sierra Leone." This turn of events completely frustrated efforts by military coup leaders to portray their country as stable and gain western support. A new government had been formed, but the rebel war was still going on.

Peace Corps did return for a short time, only to pull out again, this time for good, when the uprisings began to increase. Rebel forces became rampant in the provincial districts and along the key routes connecting Freetown with the provinces. They began to ambush vehicles which often resulted in the killing of passengers or burning of vehicles, or both. This civil war crippled the Sierra Leone economy and the cost of living rose sharply.

Unfortunately, news about the situations in Sierra Leone filtered out very slowly on this side of the world. I received a few letters from my former principal, Mr. Senessie, and at one point it looked like conditions were improving. He had been forced to closed the school in

Taiama during the heavy fighting. However, after many months of interaction with the new

Sierra Leone government, funds had been provided for rehabilitation and re-opening of the school. During this short period of peacefulness, I was able to send Mr. Senessie boxes of clothing and supplies for the people of Sierra Leone.

This good news was short-lived. A few months later, the war broke out again! In less than seven months under the new regime, the rebels had returned and invaded Freetown, the capital. The new president had to flee to Guinea. Extensive damage was done to the city of Freetown. In addition, hundreds of Sierra Leoneans had been killed or wounded and many of them evacuated to Guinea.

During this military coup, the people of Sierra Leone underwent horrible living conditions. There was massive looting, destruction of state infrastructure, commandeering of state, institutional and private vehicles, indiscriminate raping on a day to day basis, armed robbery, and maiming and slaughtering of innocent people. All of the commercial banks had closed and people were beginning to experience scarcity of food. And once again, all the schools had closed. The future of Sierra Leone was uncertain.

Over the next few years, I received a few letters from Mr. Senessie, but I had lost contact with Peter, my first student whom I had sponsored, Dominic, my second student, and Fred Ngaima, my language instructor. In 1996, conditions in Sierra Leone took an extreme turn-around again and Mr. Senessie finally had to flee to Guinea with his family.

In retrospect, one would not think that there was so much strife in Sierra Leone if you stayed in the villages all the time. Here, even though the people were extremely poor, they did not seem al all dejected. It was only when I went to Freetown and saw the abject misery in that heavily populated city, that I became angry and upset. It was there that I really saw Sierra Leone, a country crumbling in poverty and decay. After thirty-one years of independence, thirty-one years of laboring, the country was now groveling in degradation. Seemingly, the government had not served the interests of its people well. Seemingly, many of the various Missions that had come into the country had also failed.

Signs of decay were evident everywhere. Electricity was there, but the power went off frequently and without any advance notice. Water running from communal taps on street corners was polluted. Paved roads were crumbling into rocky paths under the wheels of battered minivans and other vehicles. Beggars could be seen on practically every street. Little bedraggled children, unable to go to school, wandered through the streets daily.

The inequities of the system were also evident because one would also see luxurious Mercedes and other fine vehicles being driven in the city. The owners, many who were well-to-do Africans, usually were part of the government. Others were comfortable expatriates who were working in the country, exploiting the Africans and living in grand style on the outskirts and in the high hills where luxury abounded.

Sierra Leone ranks 94th out of 102 nations in terms of living standards. For example, on the UN scale, with the United States used as a basis for comparison, with a score of 100, Sierra Leone's score is 3. The average life expectancy is 39 years of age for men, 43 for women. More than 150 of every 1000 children die in infancy. Women bear an average of six children each, and about 4 of every 1000 women die in childbirth. About two thirds of the country's residents live below the absolute poverty line. This is the level defined by the UN as the income level below which people cannot afford minimal food and other necessities.

About 85% of the population of Sierra Leone is illiterate. Only about 15% of the country's children reach secondary school. The government spends millions on itself, while education and health rank very low on the government's list of priorities.

The country is rich in diamonds and gold, but much of its mineral wealth is smuggled out of the country, and the foreigners continue to exploit and reap the benefits.

In early 1999, I received correspondence from Fred, my language instructor. He told me about the terrible conditions in Sierra Leone, and how he had escaped death a number of times. I responded to his letter, but by this time, all mail to Sierra Leone had been curtailed and my letters were returned. In fact, I received a few more letters from Fred, but again, I was unable to send mail to him on this end.

Good news! I received a letter from Peter Conteh, my first student. He was in Freetown, safe and sound. One of his brothers had been killed during the heavy fighting. I tried to reply to his letter, but again, no mail on this end was going through. I can only hope that he is still alive and well.

The year 2000—Blessings and more blessings! I received correspondence from Mr. Senessie, the principal of Taiama. He and his family are in the United States! Through the grace of a government lottery drawing whereby people are able to leave the country, they were recipients of such a lottery. As of this writing, Mr. Senessie and his family are doing well in the states.

Sadly, conditions in Sierra Leone are still critical. The fighting continues with massive destruction and maiming of citizens. Although UN forces have come into the country to try peace negotiations, the fighting has not ceased. I continue to pray for the people of Sierra Leone and hope that peace will eventually come to that country.

SIERRA LEONE
NATIONAL
ANTHEM

****

High we exalt thee, land of the free
Great is the love we have for thee.
Firmly united, ever we stand
Singing thy praise, Oh native land.

We raise up our hearts, and our voices on high
The hills and the valleys re-echo our cry.
Blessing and peace be ever thine own
Land that we love, our Sierra Leone

DR. JAMES O. PERRY–AT THE MARKET, SIERRA LEONE

AMBASSADOR CYNTHIA S. PERRY
SIGNING IN AS AMBASSADOR TO BURUNDI

Sierra Leone

AMBASSADOR PERRY WITH FRIENDS

Kenya Reunion

33

It had been 12 years since I last made a trip to Kenya and, miraculously, I got a chance to visit again. In mid October 1999, I was surprised to receive a letter from the Rev. John Githiga of St. Georges's Episcopal Church, Canyon, Texas. I did not know Rev. Githiga, and wondered why he was writing to me. I later discovered that he saw my name on a list of volunteers who had served with the Episcopal Church Diocese of New York on a mission to Panama in 1994. Having once served in Panama himself, he was interested in contacting other volunteers.

Rev. Githiga is originally a native of Kenya. He now resides in Texas and is the priest at St. George's Episcopal Church. He told me about a mission project he was conducting in February, 2000. It was a 10-day mission to Thika, Kenya, involving support and service for the Diocese of Thika. It also entailed visiting churches, missions, orphanages, and several historical sites. In addition, there would be conferences and participation in a one-day retreat. Now, the town of Thika is only a few miles from the town of Ruaraka where the new National Youth Service Secretarial College is located. What a great opportunity this was! A chance to visit the school and also reunite with some of my former students and friends. Two of my former students were still teaching at the school, and several others were living and working in nearby vicinities. What a golden opportunity! Of course I joined the mission!

When I made my travel plans for the trip to Kenya, I decided to add an additional two weeks to my itinerary. This would enable me to spend some time with my former students and friends. The missionary party consisted of five people, Rev. Githiga, Rev. Caroline Volentine, Ms. Timi Williams, Mr. Terry Bourgeois, and myself. We departed for Kenya on February 20, 2000 and arrived at Kenyatta International Airport on February 21, 2000.

I had previously written to a few of my students and Mr. Mburu to let them know that I was coming to Kenya. I had also informed them that my plane would be arriving very late in the evening, so I did not expect any of them to meet me. Imagine my surprise when I came through customs. Rev. Githiga and the rest of our missionary party were met by Bishop Gideon Githiga of Thika. I was greeted by Mr. Mburu, four of my former students, namely, Florence Nekesa, Treza Maina, Esther Kahiga and Eunice Kimani. Also two children, Rainette and Joy, and a few more friends. They presented me with bouquets of flowers, so many that I shared them with my missionary party when we arrived at our destination in Thika. What a glorious feeling I had when I saw them at the airport! I could hardly believe it!

After exchanging greetings, prayers, and joyful memories, I had to leave with my missionary party for our ten-day mission in Thika. I had made arrangements to spend two weeks at the Utali Hotel after completion of my mission, and would join my Kenyan friends on March 1st. The hotel was directly across the street from the secretarial school, so contact with them would be easily accessible.

We, the missionary party, were hosted by Bishop Gideon Githiga during our stay in Thika. We stayed at various hotels, adjacent to the sites we visited. Our mission also included a trip to St. Paul's

Theological College, in Limuru, a tour of Leakey's archaeological site, and a trip to view the Great Rift Valley in Nakuru. We made a special and heartwarming visit to St. Nicholas' Children's Home, also in Nakuru. Here we were greeted by the children of the home who performed songs and dances for our benefit. In turn, our mission party presented monetary donations to the home to help them purchase many of the items they were in dire need of, such as clothing, furnishings and other supplies. I committed myself to a donation of 100 T-shirts for the children of St. Nicholas' home which was sent to them upon my return to the United States.

Our missionary party participated in a clergy retreat and evangelistic convention for five days. Prior to the conclusion of the convention, each one in our party gave a presentation to the clergy which included African-American spirituality, the prison ministry, American-Indian spirituality, and ministry in the new millennium. When our mission ended, I was transported to Utali Hotel by clergy members. This trip also included the rest of the missionary party who were returning to the United States on the same day that I left for Ruaraka, and they proceeded on to the airport after dropping me off at the hotel.

Again, even though the hour of my arrival was late, Mr. Mburu and some of the students were waiting for me at the hotel when I arrived. We exchanged greetings, took refreshments at the hotel, and made plans for rest of my visit to Kenya. I was exhausted, but still excited about my return "home."

The rest of my visit to Kenya was a whirlwind experience. Every day, one or two of my former students came to visit me at the hotel. Mr. Mburu, forever faithful, was there each day to make plans for different activities. Florence Nekesa still taught typing at the school and resided at premises located adjacent to the school, and she, also, was there every day after her classes ended. Eunice Kimani, was still teaching English, and had added computer courses to her teaching skills. I spent a beautiful day at her home with her husband and children.

I spent a full day with Purity Nyambura, now owner of a convenience store. I attended the Methodist church where she and her family are members. Although most of the church members spoke very little English, I was asked to speak, and my presentation was translated into Kikuyu by one of the church members. Purity's two sons, whom I had not seen since they were infants, are now successful students aiming for college and greater honors.

The next stop was a day long visit at the home of Margaret Kimana Kabiru. Margaret, too, is a successful homemaker, having retired early from her position at a local bank. At her home, I was given the traditional serving of goat meat with all the trimmings, an honor that is usually reserved for special guests. This was staged by her father, mother, sister, brothers, and family offspring. Mr. Mburu accompanied me on this visit. What a wonderful day it was.

The next momentous occasion was a visit to the National Youth Service Secretarial College. Although I had seen the new school when it was dedicated in 1983, it was even more impressive now. An interesting fact also was that now the school was open to men, and I noted that some were enrolled in the typing classes. The teaching staff is composed of all Kenyans, fully qualified with excellent teaching credentials. The curriculum at the school covers extensive computer courses.

A few of my former students accompanied me when I visited the secretarial school.

Treza Maina Gichuiya gave motivational speeches in a few of the classrooms. Margaret Kimani Kabiru also gave encouraging words to the students, reflecting on the accomplishments that she and other students had made in the past when the secretarial school first began.

At the completion of our tour, we met with the Deputy Director of Education and discussed various aspects of the school. During our discussion, Treza made a proposal to the Deputy Director that the National Youth Service secretarial students be given the opportunity to sit for Pitman exams, which had not been done in the past supposedly because the school is a government school. When Treza first introduced this proposal, it appeared that it was not going to go through. Since my return to the states, however, things have changed. I received encouraging news from Treza in June, 2000, informing me that the proposal was now a reality. This was quite an accomplishment!

My reunion in Kenya continued on at a tremendous pace. Next stop, a reunion luncheon that the students had planned especially for me. This was held at the Utali Hotel, and was attended by students and faculty members. The entire luncheon and program was planned by Alice Njuguna, Mr. Mburu's oldest daughter who is employed at Utali Hotel. As with everything else, this, too, was outstanding.

Of course I had to spend a full day with Florence Nekesa at her home. As previously mentioned, Florence had named her first born after me. Rainette (who is now 20 years old) and I spent an afternoon together shopping in the city of Nairobi. She is a charming young lady now, still attending school and doing well in her subjects.

I also spent a day at Mr. Mburu's home, having dinner with his family. He has a grandchild who is five years old, also named Rainette. It was my first time seeing this second Rainette, who is also sweet and charming. I was thrilled to meet her for the first time.

The Sunday before I departed from Kenya, I attended All Saints Episcopal Church, which is located in the city of Nairobi. Mr. Mburu is a member of this church, so I was accompanied by him. We took the local bus to town, and really things had not changed very much. The bus was still very fast, even more bumpy because the roads in Kenya have deteriorated, but we arrived safely. When I arrived at the church, I was impressed by its elegance. I was also amazed to see so many Africans. When I attended All Saints, more than 20 years ago, the congregation had been predominantly white. Now, the church makeup is comprised of thousands of Africans. The service was similar to our service in the states, only, to me, more elegant and awesome.

Another encouraging factor with regard to the success of the secretarial school stems from further correspondence that I have since received from Treza. Before I completed my visit to Kenya, I had urged her and some of the former students to act as role models for the present students. I asked them to continue to keep in touch with the students at the secretarial school and thus inspire them to reach higher goals. Since my return home, Treza participated in a presentation to graduates and continuing students, teachers, principals, and secretarial school officials at the annual Secretarial Induction Seminar.

From her report, I gather that this was a presentation of wide range, with an audience of more than 200 people. Treza was received with overwhelming applause and enthusiasm. She touched on the beginning of the secretarial school and the struggles that she and the other students had encountered, but succeeded in overcoming. She stressed the importance of education and the realistic goals that could be achieved. The Director of the National Youth Service responded with a fine letter of thanks and appreciation to Treza.

It gives me a warm and grateful feeling to know that my recent visit to Kenya had some impact on the continued progress of the secretarial college.

REUNION AT JOMO KENYATTA AIRPORT
FEBRUARY 21, 2000

THE NATIONAL YOUTH SERVICE
SECRETARIAL COLLEGE—YEAR 2000

REUNION RECEPTION IN KENYA
MARCH 8, 2000

RAINETTE MIKISI
(20 YEARS OLD)

WITH RAINETTE WANGECHI
(5 YEARS OLD)

Reflections

34

To have fulfilled my dreams of going to Africa is something I shall always cherish. To see the strength and endurance of the African people through poverty, illness and sorrow is something to behold! To have been instrumental in helping the African children further their education gives me a great sense of pride. To witness the discipline of the students and see their strong desire to learn was phenomenal!

I can only continue to stress to the American children what great advantages they have in their country compared to the children of Africa. The American child does not have to see their parents struggling to get school fees together for their education. Education in the elementary and secondary schools in the United States is free. Yet, many of the American children, especially black American children, drop out of school and do not take advantage of these free educational opportunities.

I believe that if the American child were actually able to see these Africans struggle to get an education, our drop-out rate would not be so high. I can only try to emphasize and stress again and again the importance of pursuing one's education, and the wonderful advantages we have here in America. "Educate the child, you educate a family" is a common saying in the country of Kenya.

The purpose of this book is not just to record my memoirs. I truly feel that my first experience in Kenya, was, in essence, the "best years of my life." The short stay in Iran, although traumatic, was enlightening. The venture to Sierra Leone, even though short, was another "home" to me. My experiences in these countries will always be etched in my mind. The tranquility and happiness in Kenya and Sierra Leone with my fellow Africans always gave me a warm feeling of belonging there.

My native home is the United States. Were it not for the opportunities presented to me by the United States Peace Corps, I would not have been able to reach the goals that I did in these countries. Nor would I ever have been able to carry on without the presence of God guiding me.

Here, I would go so far as to encourage and urge the young black American to join the United States Peace Corps. We are needed in many countries, not just Africa. The percentage of black Americans in the Peace Corps is very small, about 12 percent. . A good time to join the Peace Corps would be after completion of undergraduate or graduate school. If the student could just sacrifice two years after graduating, before going into full-time employment, it would be worthwhile and of tremendous value. I know it may mean a monetary sacrifice, but this challenge and experience is worth more than all the money in the world.

The year 2000 marks more than 26 years since my first trip to Kenya, East Africa. Although I made many trips to Africa after completion of my Peace Corps assignment, I looked forward to the Kenya reunion in 2000. To once again view the breathtaking African savannas, to take in the beauty of Africa, which, to me, is more beautiful, if not the most beautiful continent in the world. To see the African men, women, and children walking tall, erect and proud, while facing all odds against poverty, illness, and hunger.

I enjoyed walking down the streets of Kenya once again, having the Africans greet me warmly with "Jambo" or "Habari, Mama" as they passed me on the road, not even knowing me, but just greeting me as a friend or "sister."

To see the innocent young children of Africa with hope in their faces, somewhat pathetic, but also sweet and gentle; a hope that makes you want to reach out to them. Once more I was able to mingle with the masses of black people where I was not a minority but a majority of the population. Hopefully, I will make another venture some day; this time to Madagascar, where my roots originated, and perhaps, even there, I will be able to reach out to others.

www.ingramcontent.com/pod-product-compliance
Lightning Source LLC
Chambersburg PA
CBHW061355280526
45784CB00001B/266